Followers of the Way

A Passover Haggadah

With explanations, cultural items and set up instructions

Michael Harvey Koplitz

Table of Contents

Why another Haggadah?

There are many Haggadim in the marketplace today. It is not uncommon for different synagogues and groups of Jews to create their version of the Haggadah. This version is from the Ashkenazi version which came from http://sefaria.org.

The formatting will allow the Seder participants at the Seder to follow along. The directions are in italics. Cultural references have been added to the Haggadah, along with definitions. The definitions are italicized. This Haggadah includes information about getting ready to hold a Seder.

A brief explanation of what Pesach is all about is included. Different pictures have been added to the text to make it more visually appealing.

Hopefully, this Haggadah will bless Seders for years to come. May the LORD continue to bless His people Israel from now and to eternity. Amen.

What is Passover?

Passover (Pesach) commemorates the emancipation of the Israelites from slavery in ancient Egypt._Pesach is observed by avoiding leaven, and highlighted by the <u>Seder</u> meals that include four cups of wine, eating matzah and bitter herbs, and retelling the story of the Exodus.

The Hebrew name for it is Pesach (which means "to pass over"), as Gd passed over the Jewish homes during the killing of the Egyptian firstborn on the very first Passover eve.

A Summary of the Passover story

As told in the Bible, after many decades of slavery to the Egyptian pharaohs, during which the Israelites were subjected to backbreaking labor and unbearable horrors, <u>G-d</u> saw the people's distress and sent Moses to Pharaoh with a message: "Send forth My people, so that they may serve Me." But despite numerous warnings, Pharaoh refused to heed G-d's command. G-d then sent upon Egypt ten devastating plagues, afflicting them and destroying everything from their livestock to their crops.

At the stroke of midnight of 15 Nissan in the year 2448 from creation (1313 BCE), G-d visited the last of the ten plagues on the Egyptians, killing all their firstborn. While doing so, G-d spared the children of Israel, "passing over" their homes—hence the name of the holiday. Pharaoh's resistance was broken, and he virtually chased his former slaves out of the land. The Israelites left in such a hurry, in fact, that the bread they baked as provisions for the way did not have time to rise. Six hundred thousand adult males, plus many more women and children, left Egypt on that day and began the trek to Mount Sinai and their birth as G-d's chosen people.

In ancient times, the Passover observance included the sacrifice of the paschal lamb, which was roasted and eaten at the Seder on the first night of the holiday. This was the case until the Temple in Jerusalem was destroyed in the 1st century. [1]

[1] https://www.chabad.org/holidays/passover/pesach_cdo/aid/871715/jewish/What-Is-Passover-Pesach.htm

A Summary of the Passover story

"As told in the Bible, after many decades of slavery to the Egyptian pharaohs, during which the Israelites were subjected to backbreaking labor and unbearable horrors, G-d saw the people's distress and sent Moses to Pharaoh with a message: "Send forth My people, so that they may serve Me." But despite numerous warnings, Pharaoh refused to heed G-d's command. G-d then sent upon Egypt ten devastating plagues, afflicting them and destroying everything from their livestock to their crops.

At the stroke of midnight of 15 Nissan in the year 2448 from creation (1313 BCE), G-d visited the last of the ten plagues on the Egyptians, killing all their firstborn. While doing so, G-d spared the children of Israel, "passing over" their homes—hence the name of the holiday. Pharaoh's resistance was broken, and he virtually chased his former slaves out of the land. The Israelites left in such a hurry, in fact, that the bread they baked as provisions for the way did not have time to rise. Six hundred thousand adult males, plus many more women and children, left Egypt on that day and began the trek to Mount Sinai and their birth as G-d's chosen people.

In ancient times, the Passover observance included the sacrifice of the paschal lamb, which was roasted and eaten at the Seder on the first night of the holiday. This was the case until the Temple in Jerusalem was destroyed in the 1st century."[2]

---

[2] 1. What is passover (Pesach)? - passover 2022 will be celebrated from April 15-23 - Passover, accessed April 18, 2024, https://www.chabad.org/holidays/passover/pesach_cdo/aid/871715/jewish/What-Is-Passover-Pesach.htm.

History – How did Israel Get to Egypt

According to Genesis, Joseph's ten brothers sold him to a Midian caravan which was headed toward Egypt. Pharaoh's court bought Joseph as a slave.

The identity of the Pharaoh during Joseph's time in Egypt remains uncertain, leading scholars to engage in much debate.

One theory is that the Hyksos, who were Semitic kings, were on good terms with the Hebrews. These people may have been in Northern Egypt at the time of Joseph.

From the early second millennium B.C.E., people from Canaan infiltrated the northeastern regions of Egypt. In the period known as the Second Intermediate Period (c. 1750–1550 B.C.E.), the Canaanites who had been living in the region had expanded and taken over much of the eastern Nile Delta.

This would explain why Pharaoh would make Joseph his number two. Joseph was a Semite and would have been recognized as a kissing cousin to the Hyksos. This would also explain why Pharaoh said to Joseph to bring his family to Egypt during the famine. In addition, Pharaoh gave Joseph's family part of the Goshen territory, which was the best land in all of Egypt.

History – How did Israel become slaves?

The book of Exodus says that a new Pharaoh came to power who did not know Joseph. This would correspond when the southern Egyptians, who invaded the north and forced the Hyksos to flee northern Egypt. The Hebrew people were in communities in Goshen and did not leave in mass at that point. There were probably some Israelites who left, however, we have no records to show any kind of Exodus.

The Egyptians needed workers to build the cities, especially the ones that they destroyed by invading the north. They also noticed a huge population of Semitic people they needed to control. Their decision was to take these people and make them slaves to the Egyptian government.

History - How long was Israel in Egypt?

This is a number that most people get wrong because they base it on the verse where God says to Abraham that his descendants would live in a land not their own for 400 years. The actual number of years that Israel were slaves in Egypt was 270. Abraham, Isaac, and Jacob lived in Canaan for 130 years, a land that was not their own.

Passover Seder Plate

The Passover Seder plate is a key element in the Passover Seder, holding six symbolic items that each represent aspects of the Exodus story.

- **Matzah:** Symbolizes the haste in which the Israelites left Egypt, not allowing their bread to rise.
- **Zeroa (Shankbone)**: Represents the paschal lamb sacrifice made the night the Israelites left Egypt.
- **Beitzah (Egg):** A symbol of mourning and the cycle of life.
- **Maror (Bitter Herbs)**: Reflects the bitterness of slavery the Israelites endured in Egypt.
- **Charoset (Paste)**: Symbolizes the mortar used by the Israelites when they were slaves building for the Egyptians.
- **Karpas (Vegetable):** Represents hope and renewal, dipped in salt water to recall the tears shed during slavery.

Each item on the Seder plate is deeply symbolic and integral to the retelling of the Passover story, emphasizing themes of suffering, liberation, and hope.

Why Four Cups of Wine?

The tradition of drinking four cups of wine during the Passover Seder is deeply symbolic and represents different aspects of the Exodus story. Each cup can represent the different stages of liberation: salvation from harsh labor, salvation from servitude, the splitting of the sea (after which the Jews felt completely redeemed), becoming a nation at Sinai.

Wine, considered a royal drink, symbolizes freedom, which is what the Passover Seder and Haggadah celebrate.

The Afikomen

The Afikomen is a piece of matzah that plays a significant role in the Passover Seder. Here's what it symbolizes. In ancient biblical times, the Passover sacrifice used to be the last thing consumed during the Passover Seder during the First and Second Temple eras.

To keep the children's attention during the Seder, a piece of matzah is hidden. The children at the table must search for it and bring it back after the meal. They receive a reward (usually candy, money, or a small gift) when they bring it back to the table.

After the meal and normal desserts have been eaten, each guest receives a small portion of the Afikomen, at least the size of an olive. This is done so that the last taste of the meal is matzah. After the Afikomen is eaten, the Birkas haMazon (grace after meals) is recited and the Seder is concluded.

The Elijah Cup, the Messiah, and Jesus

The Elijah cup is the hope that the Messiah will come. Jewish tradition states that the Messiah would come during the month of the Passover.

For Messianic Jews and Christians, Jesus' connection to the Passover is deeply significant in Christian theology since the Messiah has come. Jesus is often referred to as the "Passover Lamb" in Christian tradition. This refers to the belief that Jesus' death and resurrection fulfilled the symbolism of the Passover lamb's sacrifice in the Old Testament. As the apostle Paul says in 1 Corinthians 5:7, "Christ our Passover has been sacrificed".

The Last Supper, which was a Passover meal, is when Jesus instituted the Christian practice of communion. He used the unleavened bread and wine of the Passover meal to symbolize his body and blood, which would be sacrificed for the sins of humanity.

Jesus was crucified during the week of Passover. This timing is significant because it ties Jesus' death to the Passover lamb, which was sacrificed as a redemption for the sins of the people.

Jesus' death and resurrection during Passover is a fulfillment of biblical prophecy and establishes a new covenant between God and humanity.

Before you hold your Seder, you will need to follow these steps[3]

1. Cleaning

Before Passover, the house needs to be cleaned so that all chametz (leavened products) are removed. Don't forget the bag of baby crackers in your diaper bag. What about the Purim treats your 3rd grader has stashed away in her desk? Have to lift the sofa to get all that popcorn vacuumed up. While you are at it, you might as well throw some spring cleaning in there - get out the summer clothes and put away the winter blankets and coats.

2. Sabbath

Before you have looked up from the dusting, <u>Shabbat</u> HaGadol, the Shabbat before Passover, arrives. It is called Shabbat HaGadol because it marks the beginning of the redemption.

On the tenth day of the Hebrew month of Nissan (the Shabbat before the exodus on the fifteenth of Nissan), the Israelites in Egypt prepared the Passover lamb, or Pesach-lamb (Exodus 12:3). When their neighbors asked them what they were doing, the Israelites explained that the lambs would be sacrificed on the fourteenth of Nissan, just before G-d would slay the firstborn of Egypt. This frightened the firstborn children of Egypt. They begged their parents and Pharaoh to release the Israelites. When their request was denied, they rose in armed revolt. As a result, numerous enemies of the Israelites were killed.

---

[3] Katz, Lisa. "10 Easy Steps for Easy Passover Prep." Learn Religions. https://www.learnreligions.com/preparing-for-pesach-2076948 (accessed March 30, 2022).

3. Shopping

Then it's time to run to the store to get all those specialty Passover foods and products. So many kosher for Passover cakes, cookies, and cereals. One can almost last the whole week without missing chametz too much. At the same time, these specialty Passover products tend to be expensive and fattening. If you want to keep your money with you and extra pounds off you, buy extra fruits and vegetables to eat during Passover.

To minimize return trips to the store, make a careful shopping list. What will you be serving for the seder? What dishes do you plan to make during the week? Once you have your seder and weekly meals planned, try to create a shopping list that enables you to do all your Passover shopping in one stop.

4. Cooking

Now that the house is stocked, it is time to start to cook for the Seder. Better put aside at least 2 days to cook for the Seder, as many of the dishes are not ones you do every day and you may be lacking some of the accessories with which you usually cook. While cooking, be careful to keep the remaining chametz you have in the house in a separate area.

5. Selling the Chametz

We are commanded to have no chametz in our possession during Passover. Do we have to burn the closed bag of snitzel in the freezer? No. Our rabbis have made it possible for us to sell this chametz to a non-Jew prior to the holiday. Generally, we sell the chametz to a Rabbi who in turn acts as an agent and sells it to a non-Jew. The sale is real in that the non-Jew can actually get the chametz if he/she wants. And if the non-Jew decides to keep the chametz, then he/she must pay for it after the holiday.

6. Searching for Chametz

Finally, it is the night before Passover, and it is time to gather your family in your sparkling clean home for Bidikat Chametz. See our quick, step-by-step page on How to Search for Chametz. Once all the chametz in the house is found and burned, we are ready for the Passover Seder.

7. Planning the Seder

It is a good idea to put some time and thought into the kind of seder service you want. What Haggadah will you be using? There are a variety of Haggadot, including several online which can be printed, and each one has a different influence on the seder service.

Will there be children at the seder? Perhaps they can make place cards to put on the table so everyone will know where they will be sitting? Or they can make pictures of the Passover story to hang in the dining room. During the seder itself, make sure there are opportunities for the children to participate. Did the little ones practice singing the Four Questions? Did the older ones learn something about Passover at school which they can share with everyone at the table? Perhaps you can prepare some questions about the Passover story to ask the children during the seder. Is there something you can do to make the seder this year especially memorable? Our neighbor dressed up like Elijah, and when it was time to open the door for Elijah he walked in, drank the cup of wine, and left.

A few years ago, friends of mine asked all their guests to dress up like desert nomads. Then they conducted their seder on the floor as if they were in a tent in the desert.

8. Preparing the Passover Plate

It is important to prepare the six symbolic items - zeroa, beitza, karpas, maror, chazeret, charoset - which should go on the seder plate. See this quick, step-by-step page on How to Prepare the Seder Plate.

9. Setting the Passover Table

The following is needed to set the table for the Passover Seder:

- festive tablecloth and napkins
- kosher for Passover dishes, flatware, water glasses, and wine glasses
- small dishes of salt water for dipping
- enough bottles of wine and grape juice for each person to have four cups
- a special wine cup reserved for Elijah
- a plate with 3 pieces of <u>matzah</u> on it and a cover over it
- seder plate
- Haggadot

Each place setting should include a plate, flatware, a water glass, a wine glass, and a Haggadah. Soup bowls can be kept in the kitchen and used to serve the soup. The salt water dishes and wine or grape juice bottles should be spread out on the table so everyone can reach them. An empty wine glass should be placed in the middle of the table for Elijah. On the plate of the person who will lead the reading of the Haggadah, first place the plate with the three pieces of matzah, and then put the seder plate on top.

10. Pesach Kasher!

Make your seder a memorable and enjoyable experience for the whole family. A nap before the seder is recommended for all, not just the kids, so that everyone arrives to the seder with good energy and spirit. During the seder, make sure everyone is involved and feeling a part of the story of the exodus.

The Symbols of the Seder Plate

(You will need to purchase the six items that are on the Seder Plate)[4]

There are six traditional items placed on the *seder* plate, with a few modern traditions in the mix as well.

---

[4] Pelaia, Ariela. "The Symbols of the Seder Plate." Learn Religions, Aug. 28, 2020, learnreligions.com/symbols-of-the-seder-plate-2076486.

Vegetable (Karpas, כַּרְפַּס): Karpas comes from the Greek word karpos *(καρπός)*, meaning "fresh, raw vegetable."

Throughout the year, after kiddush (the blessing over wine) is recited, the first thing that's eaten is bread. On Passover, however, at the beginning of the seder meal (after kiddush) a blessing over vegetables is recited and then a vegetable – usually parsley, celery, or a boiled potato – is dipped in salt water and eaten. This prompts the table to ask Mah Nishtanah? or, "Why is this night different from all other nights?" Likewise, the salt water represents the tears the Israelites shed during their years of enslavement in Egypt.

Shank Bone (Zeroa, זְרוֹעַ): The roasted shank bone of a lamb reminds Jews of the 10th plague in Egypt when all firstborn Egyptians were killed. During this plague, the Israelites marked the doorposts of their homes with the blood of a lamb so that when Death passed over Egypt, it would pass over the Israelite homes, as it is written in Exodus 12:12:

"On that same night I will pass through Egypt and strike down every firstborn - both men and animals - and I will bring judgment on all the gods of Egypt… The blood will be a sign ... on the houses where you are; and when I see the blood, I will pass over you. No destructive plague will touch you when I strike Egypt."

The shank bone is sometimes called the Paschal lamb, with "paschal" meaning "He [God] skipped over" the houses of Israel.

The shank bone also reminds Jews of the sacrificial lamb that was killed and eaten during the days when the Temple stood in Jerusalem. In modern times, some Jews use a poultry neck, while vegetarians will often replace the shank bone with a roasted beet

(Pesachim 114b, Midrash), which has the color of blood and is shaped like a bone. In some communities, vegetarians will substitute a yam.

Roasted, Hard-Boiled Egg (Beitzah, ביצה): There are several interpretations of the symbolism of the roasted and hard-boiled egg. During the time of the Temple, a korban chagigah, or festival sacrifice, was given at the Temple and the roasted egg represents that meat offering. Also, hard boiled eggs were traditionally the first food served to mourners after a funeral, and thus the egg serves as a symbol of mourning for the loss of the two Temples (the first in 586 BCE and the second in 70 CE).

During the meal, the egg is merely symbolic, but usually, once the meal begins, people dip a hard-boiled egg in salt water as the first food of the actual meal.

Charoset (חֲרוֹסֶת): Charoset is a mixture that is often made of apples, nuts, wine, and spices in the Eastern European Ashkenazic tradition. In the Sephardic tradition, charoset is a paste made of figs, dates, and raisins. The word charoset comes from the Hebrew word cheres (חרס), meaning clay, and it represents the mortar that the Israelites were forced to use while they built structures for their Egyptian taskmasters.

Bitter Herbs (Maror, מָרוֹר): Because the Israelites were slaves in Egypt, Jews eat bitter herbs to remind them of the harshness of servitude.

"And they embittered (v'yimareru וימררו) their lives with hard labor, with mortar and with bricks and with all manner of labor in the field; any labor that they made them do was with hard labor" (Exodus 1:14).

Horseradish – either the root or a prepared paste (usually made with beets) – is most often used, although the bitter part of romaine lettuce is also very popular. Sephardic Jews tend to use green onions or curly parsley.

A small amount of maror is usually eaten with an equal portion of charoset. It can also be made into a "Hillel Sandwich," where maror and charoset are sandwiched between two pieces of matzah.

Bitter Vegetable (Chazeret, חזרת): This piece of the seder plate also symbolizes the bitterness of slavery and fulfills the requirement called korech, which is when the maror is eaten together with matzah. Romaine lettuce is usually used, which doesn't seem very bitter but the plant has bitter tasting roots. When chazeret is not represented on the seder plate some Jews will put a small bowl of salt water in its place.

Passover Haggadah starts here

Kadesh (pouring of the wine)

<u>הגדה של פסח, קדש א'-י"ג</u>

.מוזגים כוס ראשון .המצות מכוסות
קַדֵּשׁ
בְּשַׁבָּת מַתְחִילִין
וַיְהִי עֶרֶב וַיְהִי בֹקֶר יוֹם הַשִּׁשִּׁי .וַיְכֻלּוּ הַשָּׁמַיִם וְהָאָרֶץ וְכָל-צְבָאָם .וַיְכַל אֱלֹהִים בַּיּוֹם הַשְּׁבִיעִי מְלַאכְתּוֹ
אֲשֶׁר עָשָׂה וַיִּשְׁבֹּת בַּיּוֹם הַשְּׁבִיעִי מִכָּל מְלַאכְתּוֹ אֲשֶׁר עָשָׂה .וַיְבָרֶךְ אֱלֹהִים אֶת יוֹם הַשְּׁבִיעִי וַיְקַדֵּשׁ אוֹתוֹ
כִּי בוֹ שָׁבַת מִכָּל-מְלַאכְתּוֹ אֲשֶׁר בָּרָא אֱלֹהִים לַעֲשׂוֹת.
בחול מתחילין:
סַבְרִי מָרָנָן וְרַבָּנָן וְרַבּוֹתַי .בָּרוּךְ אַתָּה ה ,'אֱלֹהֵינוּ מֶלֶךְ הָעוֹלָם בּוֹרֵא פְּרִי הַגָּפֶן.
בָּרוּךְ אַתָּה ה ,'אֱלֹהֵינוּ מֶלֶךְ הָעוֹלָם אֲשֶׁר בָּחַר בָּנוּ מִכָּל-עָם וְרוֹמְמָנוּ מִכָּל-לָשׁוֹן וְקִדְּשָׁנוּ בְּמִצְוֹתָיו .וַתִּתֶּן
לָנוּ ה 'אֱלֹהֵינוּ בְּאַהֲבָה)לשבת :שַׁבָּתוֹת לִמְנוּחָה וּ (מוֹעֲדִים לְשִׂמְחָה ,חַגִּים וּזְמַנִּים לְשָׂשׂוֹן) ,לשבת :אֶת
יוֹם הַשַּׁבָּת הַזֶּה וְ (אֶת יוֹם חַג הַמַּצּוֹת הַזֶּה זְמַן חֵרוּתֵנוּ) ,לשבת :בְּאַהֲבָה (מִקְרָא קֹדֶשׁ זֵכֶר לִיצִיאַת
מִצְרָיִם .כִּי בָנוּ בָחַרְתָּ וְאוֹתָנוּ קִדַּשְׁתָּ מִכָּל הָעַמִּים) ,לשבת :וְשַׁבָּת (וּמוֹעֲדֵי קָדְשֶׁךָ)לשבת :בְּאַהֲבָה
וּבְרָצוֹן (בְּשִׂמְחָה וּבְשָׂשׂוֹן הִנְחַלְתָּנוּ.
בָּרוּךְ אַתָּה ה ,'מְקַדֵּשׁ)לשבת :הַשַּׁבָּת וְ (יִשְׂרָאֵל וְהַזְּמַנִּים.
במוצאי שבת מוסיפים:
בָּרוּךְ אַתָּה ה ,'אֱלֹהֵינוּ מֶלֶךְ הָעוֹלָם ,בּוֹרֵא מְאוֹרֵי הָאֵשׁ .בָּרוּךְ אַתָּה ה ,'אֱלֹהֵינוּ מֶלֶךְ הָעוֹלָם הַמַּבְדִּיל בֵּין
קֹדֶשׁ לְחֹל ,בֵּין אוֹר לְחֹשֶׁךְ ,בֵּין יִשְׂרָאֵל לָעַמִּים ,בֵּין יוֹם הַשְּׁבִיעִי לְשֵׁשֶׁת יְמֵי הַמַּעֲשֶׂה .בֵּין קְדֻשַּׁת שַׁבָּת

---

5 Duckduckgo.com Search 3/30/2022.

לְקַדְּשַׁת יוֹם טוֹב הִבְדַּלְתָּ, וְאֶת-יוֹם הַשְּׁבִיעִי מִשֵּׁשֶׁת יְמֵי הַמַּעֲשֶׂה קִדַּשְׁתָּ. הִבְדַּלְתָּ וְקִדַּשְׁתָּ אֶת-עַמְּךָ יִשְׂרָאֵל
בִּקְדֻשָּׁתֶךָ.
בָּרוּךְ אַתָּה ה', הַמַּבְדִּיל בֵּין קֹדֶשׁ לְקֹדֶשׁ.
בָּרוּךְ אַתָּה ה', אֱלֹהֵינוּ מֶלֶךְ הָעוֹלָם, שֶׁהֶחֱיָנוּ וְקִיְּמָנוּ וְהִגִּיעָנוּ לַזְּמַן הַזֶּה.
שׁוֹתֶה בַּהֲסִיבַת שְׂמֹאל וְאֵינוּ מְבָרֵךְ בְּרָכָה אַחֲרוֹנָה.

(Directions: The leader tells everyone to pour the first cup. The matzot are uncovered.)

(Directions: On Sabbath, begin here)

And there was evening and there was morning, the sixth day. And the heaven and the earth were finished, and all their host. And on the seventh day God finished His work which He had done; and He rested on the seventh day from all His work which He had done. And God blessed the seventh day, and sanctified it; because He rested on it from all of His work which God created in doing (Genesis 1:31-2:3).

(On weekdays, begin here:)

Blessed are You, Lord our God, King of the universe, who creates the fruit of the vine. Blessed are You, Lord our God, King of the universe, who has chosen us from all peoples and has raised us above all tongues and has sanctified us with His commandments. And You have given us, Lord our God, [Sabbaths for rest], appointed times for happiness, holidays and special times for joy, [this Sabbath day, and] this Festival of Matzot, our season of freedom [in love] a holy convocation in memory of the Exodus from Egypt. For You have chosen us and sanctified us above all peoples. In Your gracious love, You granted us Your [holy Sabbath, and] special times for happiness and joy.
Blessed are You, O Lord, who sanctifies [the Sabbath,] Israel, and the appointed times.

(Directions: On Saturday night add the following two paragraphs:)

Blessed are You, Lord our God, King of the universe, who creates the light of the fire.

Blessed are You, Lord our God, King of the universe, who distinguishes between the holy and the profane, between light and darkness, between Israel and the nations, between the seventh day and the six working days. You have distinguished between the holiness of the Sabbath and the holiness of the Festival, and You have sanctified the seventh day above the six working days. You have distinguished and sanctified Your people Israel with Your holiness.

Blessed are You, O Lord, who distinguishes between the holy and the holy.

Blessed are You, Lord our God, King of the universe, who has granted us life and sustenance and permitted us to reach this season.

(Directions: Drink while reclining to the left and do not recite a blessing after drinking.)

(Culture: Why are we supposed to recline to the left? Reclining while sitting and having a meal was done by free people. The Israelites were slaves to the Egyptians and could not do this. The action is a reminder that we are a free people. Salvation was brought to the people by the LORD through Moses and the Ten plagues. The left recline is because for most people food was held in the right hand. Leaning to the right while eating can cause chocking.)

Urchatz (washing of hands)

וּרְחַץ
"נוטלים את הידים ואין מברכים "עַל נְטִילַת יָדָיִם

(Directions: *Wash your hands but do not said the blessing "on the washing of the hands."*)

6

https://3.bp.blogspot.com/_11Ys6wmW_BM/S5m9JmP1kvI/AAAAAAAAA10/3kI2V7MxoAY/s320/Lateral+Recliner.jpg

[7] https://www.haggadot.com/uploads/clips/164648/wash-hands.jpg. Accessed 3/30/2022.

(Culture: Before a ritual as important as the Passover celebration, the hands need to be washed for two reasons. The first is hygiene. Since the hands will be touching food, washing is essential. The second reason is that the washing is symbolic of our washing the impurities of the materialistic world off ourselves. We are supposed to imagine our souls leaving the material world and entering the spiritual world. When we celebrate Passover, we are to celebrate it with all Jews from the past, present, and future. The mystics say that all Jewish souls were at Mount Sinai when the LORD gave the Torah to the people. This thought should be in our souls at this time also. All Jews were there when the first Passover occurred.)

Karpas (the greens)

<u>הגדה של פסח ,כרפס א׳-ג׳</u>

כַּרְפַּס

לוקח מן הכרפס פחות מכזית - כדי שלא יתחייב בברכה אחרונה - טובל במי מלח ,מברך "בורא פרי האדמה", "ומכווין לפטור בברכה גם את המרור .אוכל בלא הסבה.

בָּרוּךְ אַתָּה ה ,'אֱלֹהֵינוּ מֶלֶךְ הָעוֹלָם ,בּוֹרֵא פְּרִי הָאֲדָמָה.

(*Directions: Take from the greens less than a kazayit[9] - so that you will not need to say the blessing after eating it; dip it into the salt water; said the blessing "who creates the fruit of the earth;" and have in mind that this blessing will also be for the bitter herbs. Eat without reclining.*)

Blessed are you, Lord our God, King of the universe, who creates the fruit of the earth.

---

[8] http://haggadot.com. Accessed 3/30/2022.

[9] Kezayit, k'zayit, or kezayis (Hebrew: כְּזַיִת) is a Talmudic unit of volume approximately equal to the size of an average olive. The word itself literally means "like an olive." The rabbis differ on the precise definition of the unit. Source: https://en.wikipedia.org/wiki/Kezayit

Yachatz (breaking the middle matzah) [10]

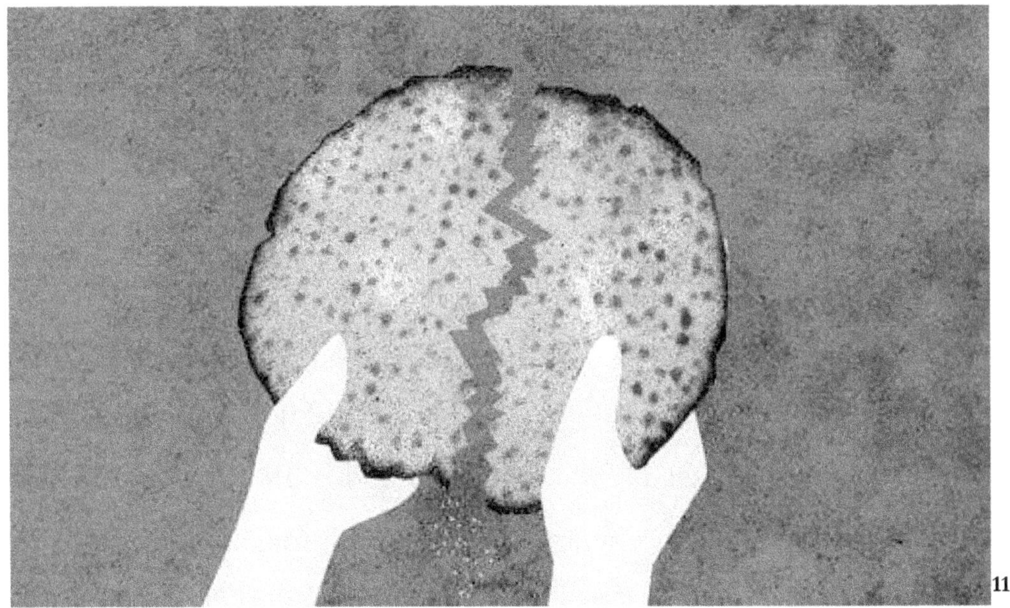

What is the Afikoman? (Hebrew: אֲפִיקוֹמָן based on Greek *epikomon* [ἐπὶ κῶμον] or *epikomion* [ἐπικώμιον], meaning "that which comes after" or "dessert"), a word originally having the connotation of "refreshments eaten after the meal", is now almost strictly associated with the half-piece of *matzo* which is broken in two during the early stages of the Passover Seder and set aside to be eaten as a dessert after the meal.

Based on the Mishnah in Pesahim 119b, the *afikoman* is a substitute for the Passover sacrifice, which was the last thing eaten at the Passover Seder during the eras of the First and Second Temples and during the period of the Tabernacle. The Talmud states that it is forbidden to have any other food after the *afikoman*, so that the taste of the *matzo* that was eaten after the meal remains in the participants' mouths. Since the destruction of the Temple and the

---

[10] https://en.wikipedia.org/wiki/Afikoman. Accessed 3/30/2022.

[11] https://www.chabad.org/holidays/passover/pesach_cdo/aid/116927/jewish/4-Yachatz-Break-the-Middle-Matzah.htm. Accessed 3/30/2022.

discontinuation of the *Korban Pesach*, Jews eat a piece of *matzo* now known as *afikomen* to finish the Passover Seder meal.

Customs around the *afikoman* vary, though they often share the common purpose of keeping children awake and alert during the Seder until the *afikoman* is eaten. Following Ashkenazi customs, the head of household may hide the *afikoman* for the children to find, or alternatively, the children may steal the *afikoman* and ransom it back. Chabad tradition discourages stealing the *afikoman* lest it lead to bad habits. Following Mizrahi customs, the *afikoman* may be tied in a sling to a child's back for the duration of the Seder.

הגדה של פסח, יחץ א'-ב'
יַחַץ
חותך את המצה האמצעית לשתים, ומצפין את הנתח הגדול לאפיקומן

(Directions: Split the middle matzah in two, and conceal the larger piece to use it for the afikoman.)

הגדה של פסח, מגיד, הא לחמא עניא א'-ג'
מַגִּיד
מגלה את המצות, מגביה את הקערה ואומר בקול רם:
הָא לַחְמָא עַנְיָא דִי אֲכָלוּ אַבְהָתָנָא בְּאַרְעָא דְמִצְרָיִם. כָּל דִכְפִין יֵיתֵי וְיֵיכֹל, כָּל דִצְרִיךְ יֵיתֵי וְיִפְסַח. הָשַׁתָּא הָכָא, לְשָׁנָה הַבָּאָה בְּאַרְעָא דְיִשְׂרָאֵל. הָשַׁתָּא עַבְדֵי, לְשָׁנָה הַבָּאָה בְּנֵי חוֹרִין.

The Recitation of the Exodus Story

(Directions: The leader uncovers the Matzot, raises the Seder plate, and says out loud.)

This is the bread of destitution that our ancestors ate in the land of Egypt. Anyone who is famished should come and eat, anyone who is in need should come and partake of the Pesach sacrifice. Now we are here, next year we will be in the land of Israel; this year we are slaves, next year we will be free people.

הגדה של פסח ,מגיד ,מה נשתנה א׳-ב׳

מסיר את הקערה מעל השולחן .מוזגין כוס שני .הבן שואל:
מַה נִּשְׁתַּנָּה הַלַּיְלָה הַזֶּה מִכָּל הַלֵּילוֹת? שֶׁבְּכָל הַלֵּילוֹת אָנוּ אוֹכְלִין חָמֵץ וּמַצָּה, הַלַּיְלָה הַזֶּה - כֻּלּוֹ מַצָּה. שֶׁבְּכָל הַלֵּילוֹת אָנוּ אוֹכְלִין שְׁאָר יְרָקוֹת - הַלַּיְלָה הַזֶּה (כֻּלּוֹ מָרוֹר). שֶׁבְּכָל הַלֵּילוֹת אֵין אָנוּ מַטְבִּילִין אֲפִילוּ פַּעַם אֶחָת - הַלַּיְלָה הַזֶּה שְׁתֵּי פְעָמִים. שֶׁבְּכָל הַלֵּילוֹת אָנוּ אוֹכְלִין בֵּין יוֹשְׁבִין וּבֵין מְסֻבִּין - הַלַּיְלָה הַזֶּה כֻּלָּנוּ מְסֻבִּין.

The Four Questions

The Explanation of the Four Questions[13]

The Four Questions are an important part of the Passover seder that highlight how Passover customs and foods distinguish the holiday from other times of the year. The youngest person at the table traditionally recited them during the fifth part of the *seder*, Maggid, which is the retelling of the Israelite exodus from Egyptian persecution found in the Passover *haggadah*.

Meaning and Origins

Called "The Four Questions" in English, the basic Hebrew question is *Mah Nishtanah ha'Lilah ha'Zeh?* which translates to "How is this night different from

---

[12] http://www.bimbam.com/wp-content/uploads/2017/02/4questions-1.png. Accessed 3/30/2021.
[13] Gordon-Bennett, Chaviva. "What Are the Four Questions at the Passover Seder?" Learn Religions. https://www.learnreligions.com/four-questions-at-the-passover-seder-4038588 (accessed March 30, 2022).

all other nights?" Then there are four verses that explain why this night is different. (Read more about the significance of the number four in Judaism.)

The questions find their origins in the Mishnah Pesachim 10:4 but appear differently in the Jerusalem (Yerushalmi) and Babylonian (Bavli) Talmud.

The Babylonian Talmud focuses on four essential questions:

- Why is matzah eaten?
- Why is maror (bitter herbs) eaten?
- Why is roasted meat eaten?
- Why is food dipped twice?

The Jerusalem Talmud focuses on three essential questions, and it is the most commonly quoted in ancient texts:

- Why is matzah eaten?
- Why is roasted meat eaten?
- Why are foods dipped twice?

The question about roasted meat refers to the paschal sacrifice that was fire roasted during the time of the Holy Temple. However, after the destruction of the Second Temple in 70 C.E., sacrifices were no longer consumed, so the question was dropped from the Passover seder questions. Later, the fourth question was added, as the number four plays a significant role in Judaism and the seder overall (see below).

The Questions

This portion of the seder *begins as the question is asked:*

Mah nishtanah ha'lilah ha'zeh mikol ha'leilot?

מַה נִּשְׁתַּנָּה הַלַּיְלָה הַזֶּה מִכָּל הַלֵּילוֹת

Why is this night different from all other nights?

The first verse is then:

She'bakol ha'leilot anu ochlin chametz u'matzah; ha'lailah ha'zeh, kuloh matzah.

שֶׁבְּכָל הַלֵּילוֹת אָנוּ אוֹכְלִין חָמֵץ וּמַצָּה הַלַּיְלָה הַזֶּה, כֻּלוֹ מַצָּה

On all other nights we eat leavened products and matzah, and on this night
only matzah.

The second verse is:

She'bakol ha'leilot anu ochlin sh'ar yerakot; ha'lailah ha'zeh, maror.

שֶׁבְּכָל הַלֵּילוֹת אָנוּ אוֹכְלִין שְׁאָר יְרָקוֹת הַלַּיְלָה הַזֶּה, כֻּלוֹ מָרוֹר

On all other nights we eat all vegetables, and on this night only bitter herbs.

The third verse is:

She'bakol ha'leilot ein anu matbilin afilu pa'am echat; ha'lailah ha'zeh, shtei
f'amim.

שֶׁבְּכָל הַלֵּילוֹת אֵין אָנוּ מַטְבִּילִין אֲפִילוּ פַּעַם אֶחָת הַלַּיְלָה הַזֶּה, שְׁתֵּי פְעָמִים

On all other nights, we don't dip our food even once, and on this night we dip
twice.

The fourth verse is:

She'bakol ha'leilot anu ochlin bein yoshvin u'vein m'subin; ha'lailah ha'zeh, kulanu m'subin.

שֶׁבְּכָל הַלֵּילוֹת אָנוּ אוֹכְלִין בֵּין יוֹשְׁבִין וּבֵין מְסֻבִּין הַלַּיְלָה הַזֶּה, כֻּלָּנוּ מְסֻבִּין

On all other nights we eat sitting or reclining, and on this night we only recline.

Although this is the most common order of the Mah Nishtanah questions, the custom of Chabad-Lubavitch, Sephardic, Mizrahi, and Yemenite communities follows the following pattern:

1. Dipping.
2. Matzah.
3. Bitter herbs.
4. Reclining.

Meaning

Each of the first three "questions" refers to a food or act of the Passover seder. Leavened bread is forbidden throughout the holiday, bitter herbs are eaten to remind us of the bitterness of slavery, and vegetables are dipped in salt water to remind us of the tears of slavery.

The fourth "question" refers to the ancient custom of eating while reclining on the left elbow and eating with the right hand. According to Maimonides (also called Rambam or Rabbi Moshe ben Maimon), this is "In the manner that kings and important people eat" (*Mishnah Pesachim*). It symbolizes the concept of freedom, that Jews would be able to have a celebratory meal while relaxing together and enjoying one another's company. As mentioned above, this fourth question was added after the destruction of the Second Temple in 70 C.E. and replaced the pre-existing question about why roasted meat is eaten during the Passover *seder*.

(Direction: He removes the plate from the table. We pour a second cup of wine. The son then asks.)

(Culture: At many Seders the youngest child who can read is the one who asks the questions. In a more traditional household the four questions would be read in Hebrew. The adults at the table should already know about the story of the Exodus. The story and its traditions are passed down through the generations at the Seder. It does not hurt the adults to remember why the Passover is remembered. Human events are often remembered in this manner.)

What differentiates this night from all [other] nights? On all [other] nights we eat *chamets* and matzah; this night, only matzah? On all [other] nights we eat other vegetables; tonight *marror*. On all [other] nights, we don't dip [our food], even one time; tonight [we dip it] twice. On [all] other nights, we eat either sitting or reclining; tonight we all recline.

הגדה של פסח ,מגיד ,עבדים היינו א'-ב'
מחזיר את הקערה אל השולחן .המצות תהיינה מגלות בשעת אמירת ההגדה.
עֲבָדִים הָיִינוּ לְפַרְעֹה בְּמִצְרָיִם ,וַיּוֹצִיאֵנוּ ה' אֱלֹהֵינוּ מִשָּׁם בְּיָד חֲזָקָה וּבִזְרֹעַ נְטוּיָה .וְאִלּוּ לֹא הוֹצִיא הַקָּדוֹשׁ בָּרוּךְ הוּא אֶת אֲבוֹתֵינוּ מִמִּצְרָיִם ,הֲרֵי אָנוּ וּבָנֵינוּ וּבְנֵי בָנֵינוּ מְשֻׁעְבָּדִים הָיִינוּ לְפַרְעֹה בְּמִצְרָיִם .וַאֲפִילוּ כֻּלָּנוּ חֲכָמִים כֻּלָּנוּ נְבוֹנִים כֻּלָּנוּ זְקֵנִים כֻּלָּנוּ יוֹדְעִים אֶת הַתּוֹרָה מִצְוָה עָלֵינוּ לְסַפֵּר בִּיצִיאַת מִצְרָיִם .וְכָל הַמַּרְבֶּה לְסַפֵּר בִּיצִיאַת מִצְרַיִם הֲרֵי זֶה מְשֻׁבָּח.

The answers: We were slaves in Egypt

(Directions: The Passover leader puts the plate back on the table. The Matzot should be uncovered during the saying of the Haggadah.)

We were slaves to Pharaoh in the land of Egypt. And the Lord, our God, took us out from there with a strong hand and an outstretched forearm. And if the Holy One, blessed be He, had not taken our ancestors from Egypt, behold we and our children and our children's children would [all] be enslaved to Pharaoh in Egypt. And even if we were all sages, all discerning, all elders, all knowledgeable about the Torah, it is a commandment upon us to tell the story of the exodus from Egypt. And anyone who adds [and spends extra time] in telling the story of the exodus from Egypt, behold he is praiseworthy.

הגדה של פסח ,מגיד ,מעשה שהיה בבני ברק א׳-ב׳

מַעֲשֶׂה בְּרַבִּי אֱלִיעֶזֶר וְרַבִּי יְהוֹשֻׁעַ וְרַבִּי אֶלְעָזָר בֶּן-עֲזַרְיָה וְרַבִּי עֲקִיבָא וְרַבִּי טַרְפוֹן שֶׁהָיוּ מְסֻבִּין בִּבְנֵי-בְרַק וְהָיוּ מְסַפְּרִים בִּיצִיאַת מִצְרַיִם כָּל-אוֹתוֹ הַלַּיְלָה ,עַד שֶׁבָּאוּ תַלְמִידֵיהֶם וְאָמְרוּ לָהֶם רַבּוֹתֵינוּ הִגִּיעַ זְמַן קְרִיאַת שְׁמַע שֶׁל שַׁחֲרִית.

אָמַר רַבִּי אֶלְעָזָר בֶּן-עֲזַרְיָה הֲרֵי אֲנִי כְּבֶן שִׁבְעִים שָׁנָה וְלֹא זָכִיתִי שֶׁתֵּאָמֵר יְצִיאַת מִצְרַיִם בַּלֵּילוֹת עַד שֶׁדְּרָשָׁהּ בֶּן זוֹמָא ,שֶׁנֶּאֱמַר ,לְמַעַן תִּזְכֹּר אֶת יוֹם צֵאתְךָ מֵאֶרֶץ מִצְרַיִם כֹּל יְמֵי חַיֶּיךָ. יְמֵי חַיֶּיךָ הַיָּמִים .כֹּל יְמֵי חַיֶּיךָ הַלֵּילוֹת .וַחֲכָמִים אוֹמְרִים יְמֵי חַיֶּיךָ הָעוֹלָם הַזֶּה .כֹּל יְמֵי חַיֶּיךָ לְהָבִיא לִימוֹת הַמָּשִׁיחַ:

---

[14] http://jewsofjudaism.com. Accessed 3/30/2022.

The Story of the Five Rabbis

It happened once [on Pesach] that Rabbi Eliezer, Rabbi Yehoshua, Rabbi Elazar ben Azariah, Rabbi Akiva and Rabbi Tarfon were reclining in Bnei Brak and were telling the story of the exodus from Egypt that whole night, until their students came and said to them, "The time of [reciting] the morning Shema has arrived."

Rabbi Elazar ben Azariah said, "Behold I am like a man of seventy years and I have not merited [to understand why] the exodus from Egypt should be said at night until Ben Zoma explicated it, as it is stated (Deuteronomy 16:3), 'In order that you remember the day of your going out from the land of Egypt all the days of your life;' 'the days of your life' [indicates that the remembrance be invoked during] the days, 'all the days of your life' [indicates that the remembrance be invoked also during] the nights." But the Sages say, "'the days of your life' [indicates that the remembrance be invoked in] this world, 'all the days of your life' [indicates that the remembrance be invoked also in] the next world."

הגדה של פסח, מגיד, כנגד ארבעה בנים א'-ה'

בָּרוּךְ הַמָּקוֹם, בָּרוּךְ הוּא, בָּרוּךְ שֶׁנָּתַן תּוֹרָה לְעַמּוֹ יִשְׂרָאֵל, בָּרוּךְ הוּא. כְּנֶגֶד אַרְבָּעָה בָנִים דִּבְּרָה תוֹרָה:
אֶחָד חָכָם, וְאֶחָד רָשָׁע, וְאֶחָד תָּם, וְאֶחָד שֶׁאֵינוֹ יוֹדֵעַ לִשְׁאוֹל.
חָכָם מָה הוּא אוֹמֵר? מָה הָעֵדוֹת וְהַחֻקִּים וְהַמִּשְׁפָּטִים אֲשֶׁר צִוָּה ה' אֱלֹהֵינוּ אֶתְכֶם. וְאַף אַתָּה אֱמוֹר לוֹ כְּהִלְכוֹת הַפֶּסַח: אֵין מַפְטִירִין אַחַר הַפֶּסַח אֲפִיקוֹמָן.
רָשָׁע מָה הוּא אוֹמֵר? מָה הָעֲבוֹדָה הַזֹּאת לָכֶם. לָכֶם - וְלֹא לוֹ. וּלְפִי שֶׁהוֹצִיא אֶת עַצְמוֹ מִן הַכְּלָל כָּפַר בְּעִקָּר. וְאַף אַתָּה הַקְהֵה אֶת שִׁנָּיו וֶאֱמוֹר לוֹ: "בַּעֲבוּר זֶה עָשָׂה ה' לִי בְּצֵאתִי מִמִּצְרָיִם". לִי וְלֹא-לוֹ. אִלּוּ הָיָה שָׁם, לֹא הָיָה נִגְאָל:
תָּם מָה הוּא אוֹמֵר? מַה זֹּאת? וְאָמַרְתָּ אֵלָיו "בְּחוֹזֶק יָד הוֹצִיאָנוּ ה' מִמִּצְרַיִם מִבֵּית עֲבָדִים".
וְשֶׁאֵינוֹ יוֹדֵעַ לִשְׁאוֹל - אַתְּ פְּתַח לוֹ, שֶׁנֶּאֱמַר, וְהִגַּדְתָּ לְבִנְךָ בַּיּוֹם הַהוּא לֵאמֹר, בַּעֲבוּר זֶה עָשָׂה ה' לִי בְּצֵאתִי מִמִּצְרָיִם

The Four Sons

¹⁶

Blessed is the Place [of all], Blessed is He; Blessed is the One who Gave the Torah to His people Israel, Blessed is He. Corresponding to four sons did the Torah speak; one [who is] wise, one [who is] evil, one who is innocent and one who doesn't know to ask. What does the wise [son] say? "What are these testimonies, statutes and judgments that the Lord our God commanded you?" And accordingly you will say to him, as per the laws of the Pesach sacrifice, "We may not eat an afikoman [a dessert or other foods eaten after the meal] after [we are finished eating] the Pesach sacrifice. (Mishnah Pesachim 10:8)"

What does the evil [son] say? "What is this worship to you?" 'To you' and not 'to him.' And since he excluded himself from the collective, he denied a principle [of the Jewish faith]. And accordingly, you will blunt his teeth and say to him, "'For the sake of this, did the Lord do [this] for *me* in my going out of Egypt' (Exodus 13:8)." 'For me' and not 'for him.' If he had been there, he would not have been saved.

What does the innocent [son] say? "What is this?" And you will said to him, "'With the strength of [His] hand did the Lord take us out from Egypt, from the house of slaves' (Exodus 13:14).'"

---

¹⁶ http://chabad.org . Accessed 3/30/2022.

And [regarding] the one who doesn't know to ask, you will open [the conversation] for him. As it is stated (Exodus 13:8), "And you will speak to your your son on that day saying, for the sake of this, did the Lord do [this] for me in my going out of Egypt."

<u>הגדה של פסח ,מגיד ,יכול מראש חודש א׳</u>

יָכוֹל מֵראשׁ חֹדֶשׁ ?תַּלְמוּד לוֹמַר בַּיוֹם הַהוּא .אִי בַּיוֹם הַהוּא יָכוֹל מִבְּעוֹד יוֹם ?תַּלְמוּד לוֹמַר בַּעֲבוּר זֶה -
בַּעֲבוּר זֶה לֹא אָמַרְתִּי ,אֶלָּא בְּשָׁעָה שֶׁיֵּשׁ מַצָּה וּמָרוֹר מֻנָּחִים לְפָנֶיךָ.

Yechol Me'rosh Chodesh

17

What does the Yechol Me'rosh Chodesh mean?[18]

After the pivotal section of the Seder in the Maggid station of the four sons, a short paragraph titled Yachol M'rosh Chodesh follows. This paragraph dicusses a Pasuk in Shemot Perek 13 Pasuk 8 which told us exactly when we are onligated in the telling of Yetziat Mitzraim: "'וְהִגַּדְתָּ לְבִנְךָ בַּיּוֹם הַהוּא לֵאמֹר בַּעֲבוּר זֶה עָשָׂה יְהוָה לִי"told,"צֵאתִי מִמִּצְרָיִם "saidu shall tell your son on that day, saying, 'Because of this, the Lord did [this] for me when I went out of Egypt.'" (Tanach.org).

A textual question arrives from this pasuk, what day is referred to by the words "on that day?"One might have thought that you should begin recounting the story of Yetziat Mitzrayim from the beginning of the month of Nisan for various reasons that I will go into later, but nevertheless there is a consensus that it is actually seder night where we are obligated. Moreover, Rambam said that while on one hand it makes sense to be obligated to retell the story specifically on seder night from looking at the wording of

---

[17] http://miriamswords.blogspot.com. Accessed 3/30/2022.

[18] https://www.haggadot.com/clip/yachol-mrosh-chodesh-megan. Accessed 3/30/2022.

the mitzvah-"Zachor"- to remember our redemption, which occurred on seder night, but on the other hand just like the mitzvah of Zachor with regard to Shabbat-where we begin preparing at the beginning of the week, so to here for Pesach we should begin preparing at no only the beginning of the week but the beginning of the month! However, the combination in the pasuk of "on that day" and "because of this" teaches us when exactly we should start discussing the story of Pesach. While the wording "on that day" can be interpreted that we should be told the story during the daytime, the following words "because of this" mean that there must be something tangible connected to the telling of the story and they must be together. Therefore, the time this pasuk is referring to is seder night, when we have maror and matza to help aid our discussion.

It could be from Rosh Chodesh [that one would have to observe Pesach. However] we learn [otherwise, since] it is stated, "on that day." If it is [written] "on that day," it could be from while it is still day [before the night of the fifteenth of Nissan. However] we learn [otherwise, since] it is stated, "for the sake of this." I didn't said 'for the sake of this' except [that it be observed] when [this] matzah and maror are resting in front of you [meaning, on the night of the fifteenth].

<u>הגדה של פסח ,מגיד ,מתחילה עובדי עבודה זרה היו אבותינו א'-ה'</u>

מִתְּחִלָּה עוֹבְדֵי עֲבוֹדָה זָרָה הָיוּ אֲבוֹתֵינוּ ,וְעַכְשָׁיו קֵרְבָנוּ הַמָּקוֹם לַעֲבֹדָתוֹ ,שֶׁנֶּאֱמַר :וַיֹּאמֶר יְהוֹשֻׁעַ אֶל-כָּל-הָעָם ,כֹּה אָמַר ה' אֱלֹהֵי יִשְׂרָאֵל :בְּעֵבֶר הַנָּהָר יָשְׁבוּ אֲבוֹתֵיכֶם מֵעוֹלָם ,תֶּרַח אֲבִי אַבְרָהָם וַאֲבִי נָחוֹר ,וַיַּעַבְדוּ אֱלֹהִים אֲחֵרִים.

וָאֶקַּח אֶת-אֲבִיכֶם אֶת-אַבְרָהָם מֵעֵבֶר הַנָּהָר וָאוֹלֵךְ אוֹתוֹ בְּכָל-אֶרֶץ כְּנָעַן ,וָאַרְבֶּה אֶת-זַרְעוֹ וָאֶתֶּן לוֹ אֶת-יִצְחָק ,וָאֶתֵּן לְיִצְחָק אֶת-יַעֲקֹב וְאֶת-עֵשָׂו .וָאֶתֵּן לְעֵשָׂו אֶת-הַר שֵׂעִיר לָרֶשֶׁת אֹתוֹ ,וְיַעֲקֹב וּבָנָיו יָרְדוּ מִצְרָיִם. בָּרוּךְ שׁוֹמֵר הַבְטָחָתוֹ לְיִשְׂרָאֵל ,בָּרוּךְ הוּא .שֶׁהַקָּדוֹשׁ בָּרוּךְ הוּא חִשַּׁב אֶת הַקֵּץ ,לַעֲשׂוֹת כְּמוֹ שֶׁאָמַר לְאַבְרָהָם אָבִינוּ בִּבְרִית בֵּין הַבְּתָרִים ,שֶׁנֶּאֱמַר :וַיֹּאמֶר לְאַבְרָם ,יָדֹעַ תֵּדַע כִּי-גֵר יִהְיֶה זַרְעֲךָ בְּאֶרֶץ לֹא לָהֶם ,וַעֲבָדוּם וְעִנּוּ אֹתָם אַרְבַּע מֵאוֹת שָׁנָה .וְגַם אֶת-הַגּוֹי אֲשֶׁר יַעֲבֹדוּ דָּן אָנֹכִי וְאַחֲרֵי-כֵן יֵצְאוּ בִּרְכֻשׁ גָּדוֹל.

מכסה המצה ומגביה את הכוס בידו ,ואומר:

וְהִיא שֶׁעָמְדָה לַאֲבוֹתֵינוּ וְלָנוּ. שֶׁלֹא אֶחָד בִּלְבָד עָמַד עָלֵינוּ לְכַלּוֹתֵנוּ, אֶלָּא שֶׁבְּכָל דּוֹר וָדוֹר עוֹמְדִים עָלֵינוּ לְכַלּוֹתֵנוּ, וְהַקָּדוֹשׁ בָּרוּךְ הוּא מַצִּילֵנוּ מִיָּדָם.

In the Beginning, Our Fathers Were Idol Worshipers

From the beginning, our ancestors were idol worshipers. And now, the Place [of all] has brought us close to His worship, as it is stated (Joshua 24:2-4), "Yehoshua said to the whole people, so said the Lord, God of Israel, 'over the river did your ancestors dwell from always, Terach the father of Avraham and the father of Nachor, and they worshiped other gods."

And I took your father, Avraham (Abraham) from over the river and I made him walk in all the land of Canaan and I increased his seed and I gave him Yitschak (Isaac). And I gave to Yitschak, Ya'akov (Jacob) and Esav (Esau), and I gave to Esav, Mount Seir [in order that he] inherit it; and Yaakov and his sons went down to Egypt.'"

Blessed is the One who keeps his promise to Israel, blessed be He; since the Holy One, blessed be He, calculated the end [of the exile,] to do as He said to Avraham, our father, in the Covenant between the Pieces, as it is stated (Genesis 15:13-14), "And He said to Avram, 'you should surely know that your seed will be a stranger in a land that is not theirs, and they will enslave them and afflict them four hundred years. And also that nation for which they shall toil will I judge, and afterwards they will will go out with much property.'"

---

[19] http://medium.com. Accessed 3/20/2022.

And it is this that has stood for our ancestors and for us, since it is not [only] one [person or nation] that has stood [against] us to destroy us, but rather in each generation, they stand [against] us to destroy us, but the Holy One, blessed be He, rescues us from their hand.

הגדה של פסח ,מגיד ,ארמי אבד אבי א'-כ"ד

יניח הכוס מידו ויגלה אֶת המצות.

צֵא וּלְמַד מַה בִּקֵשׁ לָבָן הָאֲרַמִּי לַעֲשׂוֹת לְיַעֲקֹב אָבִינוּ :שֶׁפַּרְעֹה לֹא גָזַר אֶלָּא עַל הַזְּכָרִים ,וְלָבָן בִּקֵשׁ לַעֲקֹר אֶת-הַכֹּל .שֶׁנֶּאֱמַר :אֲרַמִּי אֹבֵד אָבִי ,וַיֵּרֶד מִצְרַיְמָה וַיָּגָר שָׁם בִּמְתֵי מְעָט ,וַיְהִי שָׁם לְגוֹי גָּדוֹל ,עָצוּם וָרָב.

וַיֵּרֶד מִצְרַיְמָה - אָנוּס עַל פִּי הַדִּבּוּר .וַיָּגָר שָׁם .מְלַמֵּד שֶׁלֹּא יָרַד יַעֲקֹב אָבִינוּ לְהִשְׁתַּקֵּעַ בְּמִצְרַיִם אֶלָּא לָגוּר שָׁם ,שֶׁנֶּאֱמַר ,וַיֹּאמְרוּ אֶל-פַּרְעֹה ,לָגוּר בָּאָרֶץ בָּאנוּ ,כִּי אֵין מִרְעֶה לַצֹּאן אֲשֶׁר לַעֲבָדֶיךָ ,כִּי כָבֵד הָרָעָב בְּאֶרֶץ כְּנָעַן .וְעַתָּה יֵשְׁבוּ-נָא עֲבָדֶיךָ בְּאֶרֶץ גֹּשֶׁן.

בִּמְתֵי מְעָט .כְּמָה שֶׁנֶּאֱמַר :בְּשִׁבְעִים נֶפֶשׁ יָרְדוּ אֲבֹתֶיךָ מִצְרָיְמָה ,וְעַתָּה שָׂמְךָ ה 'אֱלֹהֶיךָ כְּכוֹכְבֵי הַשָּׁמַיִם לָרֹב.

וַיְהִי שָׁם לְגוֹי .מְלַמֵּד שֶׁהָיוּ יִשְׂרָאֵל מְצֻיָּנִים שָׁם .גָּדוֹל עָצוּם - כְּמָה שֶׁנֶּאֱמַר :וּבְנֵי יִשְׂרָאֵל פָּרוּ וַיִּשְׁרְצוּ וַיִּרְבּוּ וַיַּעַצְמוּ בִּמְאֹד מְאֹד ,וַתִּמָּלֵא הָאָרֶץ אֹתָם.

וָרָב .כְּמָה שֶׁנֶּאֱמַר :רְבָבָה כְּצֶמַח הַשָּׂדֶה נְתַתִּיךְ ,וַתִּרְבִּי וַתִּגְדְּלִי וַתָּבֹאִי בַּעֲדִי עֲדָיִים ,שָׁדַיִם נָכֹנוּ וּשְׂעָרֵךְ צִמֵּחַ ,וְאַתְּ עֵרֹם וְעֶרְיָה .וָאֶעֱבֹר עָלַיִךְ וָאֶרְאֵךְ מִתְבּוֹסֶסֶת בְּדָמָיִךְ ,וָאֹמַר לָךְ בְּדָמַיִךְ חֲיִי ,וָאֹמַר לָךְ בְּדָמַיִךְ חֲיִי

וַיָּרֵעוּ אֹתָנוּ הַמִּצְרִים וַיְעַנּוּנוּ ,וַיִּתְּנוּ עָלֵינוּ עֲבֹדָה קָשָׁה .וַיָּרֵעוּ אֹתָנוּ הַמִּצְרִים - כְּמָה שֶׁנֶּאֱמַר :הָבָה נִתְחַכְּמָה לוֹ פֶּן יִרְבֶּה ,וְהָיָה כִּי תִקְרֶאנָה מִלְחָמָה וְנוֹסַף גַּם הוּא עַל שֹׂנְאֵינוּ וְנִלְחַם-בָּנוּ ,וְעָלָה מִן-הָאָרֶץ.

וַיְעַנּוּנוּ .כְּמָה שֶׁנֶּאֱמַר :וַיָּשִׂימוּ עָלָיו שָׂרֵי מִסִּים לְמַעַן עַנֹּתוֹ בְּסִבְלֹתָם .וַיִּבֶן עָרֵי מִסְכְּנוֹת לְפַרְעֹה אֶת-פִּתֹם וְאֶת-רַעַמְסֵס.

וַיִּתְּנוּ עָלֵינוּ עֲבֹדָה קָשָׁה .כְּמָה שֶׁנֶּאֱמַר :וַיַּעֲבִדוּ מִצְרַיִם אֶת-בְּנֵי יִשְׂרָאֵל בְּפָרֶךְ.

וַנִּצְעַק אֶל-ה 'אֱלֹהֵי אֲבֹתֵינוּ ,וַיִּשְׁמַע ה 'אֶת-קֹלֵנוּ ,וַיַּרְא אֶת-עָנְיֵנוּ וְאֶת עֲמָלֵנוּ וְאֶת לַחֲצֵנוּ.

וַנִּצְעַק אֶל-ה 'אֱלֹהֵי אֲבֹתֵינוּ - כְּמָה שֶׁנֶּאֱמַר :וַיְהִי בַיָּמִים הָרַבִּים הָהֵם וַיָּמָת מֶלֶךְ מִצְרַיִם ,וַיֵּאָנְחוּ בְנֵי-יִשְׂרָאֵל מִ-הָעֲבוֹדָה וַיִּזְעָקוּ ,וַתַּעַל שַׁוְעָתָם אֶל-הָאֱלֹהִים מִן הָעֲבֹדָה.

וַיִּשְׁמַע ה 'אֶת קֹלֵנוּ .כְּמָה שֶׁנֶּאֱמַר :וַיִּשְׁמַע אֱלֹהִים אֶת-נַאֲקָתָם ,וַיִּזְכֹּר אֱלֹהִים אֶת-בְּרִיתוֹ אֶת-אַבְרָהָם ,אֶת-יִצְחָק וְאֶת-יַעֲקֹב.

וַיַּרְא אֶת-עָנְיֵנוּ .זוֹ פְּרִישׁוּת דֶּרֶךְ אֶרֶץ ,כְּמָה שֶׁנֶּאֱמַר :וַיַּרְא אֱלֹהִים אֶת בְּנֵי-יִשְׂרָאֵל וַיֵּדַע אֱלֹהִים.

וְאֶת-עֲמָלֵנוּ .אֵלּוּ הַבָּנִים .כְּמָה שֶׁנֶּאֱמַר :כָּל-הַבֵּן הַיִּלּוֹד הַיְאֹרָה תַּשְׁלִיכֻהוּ וְכָל-הַבַּת תְּחַיּוּן.

וְאֶת לַחֲצֵנוּ .זֶה הַדֹּחַק ,כְּמָה שֶׁנֶּאֱמַר :וְגַם-רָאִיתִי אֶת-הַלַּחַץ אֲשֶׁר מִצְרַיִם לֹחֲצִים אֹתָם.

וַיּוֹצִאֵנוּ ה 'מִמִּצְרַיִם בְּיָד חֲזָקָה ,וּבִזְרֹעַ נְטוּיָה ,וּבְמֹרָא גָּדֹל ,וּבְאֹתוֹת וּבְמֹפְתִים.

וַיּוֹצִאֵנוּ ה' מִמִּצְרַיִם. לֹא עַל-יְדֵי מַלְאָךְ, וְלֹא עַל-יְדֵי שָׂרָף, וְלֹא עַל-יְדֵי שָׁלִיחַ, אֶלָּא הַקָּדוֹשׁ בָּרוּךְ הוּא בִּכְבוֹדוֹ וּבְעַצְמוֹ. שֶׁנֶּאֱמַר: וְעָבַרְתִּי בְאֶרֶץ מִצְרַיִם בַּלַּיְלָה הַזֶּה, וְהִכֵּיתִי כָל-בְּכוֹר בְּאֶרֶץ מִצְרַיִם מֵאָדָם וְעַד בְּהֵמָה, וּבְכָל אֱלֹהֵי מִצְרַיִם אֶעֱשֶׂה שְׁפָטִים. אֲנִי ה'.

וְעָבַרְתִּי בְאֶרֶץ מִצְרַיִם בַּלַּיְלָה הַזֶּה - אֲנִי וְלֹא מַלְאָךְ; וְהִכֵּיתִי כָל בְּכוֹר בְּאֶרֶץ-מִצְרַיִם. אֲנִי וְלֹא שָׂרָף. וּבְכָל-אֱלֹהֵי מִצְרַיִם אֶעֱשֶׂה שְׁפָטִים. אֲנִי וְלֹא הַשָּׁלִיחַ; אֲנִי ה'. אֲנִי הוּא וְלֹא אַחֵר.

בְּיָד חֲזָקָה. זוֹ הַדֶּבֶר, כְּמָה שֶׁנֶּאֱמַר: הִנֵּה יַד-ה' הוֹיָה בְּמִקְנְךָ אֲשֶׁר בַּשָּׂדֶה, בַּסּוּסִים, בַּחֲמֹרִים, בַּגְּמַלִּים, בַּבָּקָר וּבַצֹּאן, דֶּבֶר כָּבֵד מְאֹד.

וּבִזְרֹעַ נְטוּיָה. זוֹ הַחֶרֶב, כְּמָה שֶׁנֶּאֱמַר: וְחַרְבּוֹ שְׁלוּפָה בְּיָדוֹ, נְטוּיָה עַל-יְרוּשָׁלָיִם.

וּבְמוֹרָא גָּדֹל. זוֹ גִּלּוּי שְׁכִינָה. כְּמָה שֶׁנֶּאֱמַר, אוֹ הֲנִסָּה אֱלֹהִים לָבוֹא לָקַחַת לוֹ גוֹי מִקֶּרֶב גּוֹי בְּמַסֹּת בְּאֹתֹת וּבְמוֹפְתִים וּבְמִלְחָמָה וּבְיָד חֲזָקָה וּבִזְרוֹעַ נְטוּיָה וּבְמוֹרָאִים גְּדֹלִים כְּכֹל אֲשֶׁר-עָשָׂה לָכֶם ה' אֱלֹהֵיכֶם בְּמִצְרַיִם לְעֵינֶיךָ.

וּבְאֹתוֹת. זֶה הַמַּטֶּה, כְּמָה שֶׁנֶּאֱמַר: וְאֶת הַמַּטֶּה הַזֶּה תִּקַּח בְּיָדְךָ, אֲשֶׁר תַּעֲשֶׂה-בּוֹ אֶת הָאֹתוֹת.

וּבְמֹפְתִים. זֶה הַדָּם, כְּמָה שֶׁנֶּאֱמַר: וְנָתַתִּי מוֹפְתִים בַּשָּׁמַיִם וּבָאָרֶץ

First Fruits Declaration

(Directions: Seder leader puts down the cup from his hand and uncovers the matzah.)

Go out and learn what what Lavan the Aramean sought to do to Ya'akov, our father; since Pharaoh only decreed [the death sentence] on the males but Lavan sought to uproot the whole [people]. As it is stated (Deuteronomy 26:5), "An Aramean was destroying my father and he went down to Egypt, and he resided there with a small number and he became there a nation, great, powerful and numerous."

"And he went down to Egypt" - helpless on account of the word [in which God told Avraham that his descendants would have to go into exile]. "And he resided there" - [this] teaches that Ya'akov, our father, didn't go down to settle in Egypt, but rather [only] to reside there, as it is stated (Genesis 47:4), "And they said to Pharaoh, to reside in the land have we come, since there is not enough pasture for your servant's flocks, since the the famine is heavy in the land of Canaan, and now please grant that your servants should dwell in the land of Goshen."

---

[20] http://glorymin.net. Accessed 3/30/2022.

"As a small number" - as it is stated (Deuteronomy 10:22), "With seventy souls did your ancestors come down to Egypt, and now the Lord your God has made you as numerous as the stars of the sky."

"And he became there a nation" - [this] teaches that Israel [became] distinguishable] there. "Great, powerful" - as it is stated (Exodus 1:7), "And the children of Israel multiplied and swarmed and grew numerous and strong, most exceedingly and the land became full of them."

"And numerous" - as it is stated (Ezekiel 16:7), "I have given you to be numerous as the vegetation of the field, and you increased and grew and became highly ornamented, your breasts were set and your hair grew, but you were naked and barren;" "And I passed over you and I saw you wallowing in your blood, and I said to you, you shall live in your blood, and I said to you, you shall live in your blood" (Ezekiel 16:6).

"And the Egyptians did bad to us and afflicted us and put upon us hard work" (Deuteronomy 26:6). "And the Egyptians did bad to us" - as it is stated (Exodus 1:10), "Let us be wise towards him, lest he multiply and it will be that when war is called, he too will join with our enemies and fight against us and go up from the land."

"And afflicted us" - as is is stated (Exodus 1:11); "And they placed upon him leaders over the work-tax in order to afflict them with their burdens, and they built storage cities, Pitom and Ra'amses."

"And put upon us hard work" - as it is stated (Exodus 1:11), "And they enslaved the children of Israel with breaking work."

"And we we yelled out to the Lord, the God of our ancestors, and the Lord heard our voice, and He saw our affliction, and our toil and our duress" (Deuteronomy 26:7).

"And we yelled out to the Lord, the God of our ancestors" - as it is stated (Exodus 1:23); "And it was in those great days that the king of Egypt died and the Children of Israel sighed from the work and yelled out, and their supplication went up to God from the work."

"And the Lord heard our voice" - as it is stated (Exodus 1:24); "And God heard their groans and God remembered his covenant with Avraham and with Yitschak and with Ya'akov."

"And He saw our affliction" - this [refers to] the separation from the way of the world, as it is stated (Exodus 1:25); "And God saw the Children of Israel and God knew."

"And our toil" - this [refers to the killing of the] sons, as it is stated (Exodus 1:24); "Every boy that is born, throw him into the Nile and every girl you shall keep alive."

"And our duress" - this [refers to] the pressure, as it is stated (Exodus 3:19); "And I also saw the duress that the Egyptians are applying on them."

"And the Lord took us out of Egypt with a strong hand and with an outstretched forearm and with great awe and with signs and with wonders" (Deuteronomy 26:8).

"And the Lord took us out of Egypt" - not though an angel and not through a seraph and not through a messenger, but [directly by] the Holy One, blessed be He, Himself, as it is stated (Exodus 12:12); "And I will pass through the land of Egypt on that night and I will smite every firstborn in the land of Egypt, from men to animals; and with all the gods of Egypt, I will make judgements, I am the Lord."

"And I will pass through the land of Egypt" - I and not an angel. "And I will smite every firstborn" - I and not a seraph. "And with all the gods of Egypt, I will make judgements" - I and not a messenger. "I am the Lord" - I am He and there is no other.

"With a strong hand" - this [refers to] the pestilence, as it is stated (Exodus 9:3); "Behold the hand of the Lord is upon your herds that are in the field, upon the horses, upon the donkeys, upon the camels, upon the cattle and upon the flocks, [there will be] a very heavy pestilence."

"And with an outstretched forearm" - this [refers to] the sword, as it is stated (I Chronicles 21:16); "And his sword was drawn in his hand, leaning over Jerusalem.

"And with great awe" - this [refers to the revelation of] the Divine Presence, as it is stated (Deuteronomy 4:34); Or did God try to take for Himself a nation from within a nation with enigmas, with signs and with wonders and with war and with a strong hand and with an outstretched forearm and with great and awesome acts, like all that the Lord, your God, did for you in Egypt in front of your eyes?"

"And with signs" - this [refers to] the staff, as it is stated (Exodus 4:17); "And this staff you shall take in your hand, that with it you will preform signs."

"And with wonders" - this [refers to] the blood, as it is stated (Joel 3:3); "And I will place my wonders in the skies and in the earth:

<u>הגדה של פסח, מגיד, עשרת המכות א׳-כ׳</u>

כשאומר דם ואש ותימרות עשן ,עשר המכות ודצ"ך עד"ש באח"ב - ישפוך מן הכוס מעט יין:

דָּם וָאֵשׁ וְתִימְרוֹת עָשָׁן.

דָּבָר אַחֵר: בְּיָד חֲזָקָה שְׁתַּיִם, וּבִזְרֹעַ נְטוּיָה שְׁתַּיִם, וּבְמֹרָא גָּדֹל - שְׁתַּיִם, וּבְאֹתוֹת - שְׁתַּיִם, וּבְמֹפְתִים שְׁתַּיִם.

אֵלּוּ עֶשֶׂר מַכּוֹת שֶׁהֵבִיא הַקָּדוֹשׁ בָּרוּךְ הוּא עַל-הַמִּצְרִים בְּמִצְרַיִם, וְאֵלּוּ הֵן:

דָּם

צְפַרְדֵּעַ

כִּנִּים

עָרוֹב

דֶּבֶר

שְׁחִין

בָּרָד

אַרְבֶּה

חֹשֶׁךְ

מַכַּת בְּכוֹרוֹת

רַבִּי יְהוּדָה הָיָה נוֹתֵן בָּהֶם סִמָּנִים: דְּצַ"ךְ עַד"שׁ בְּאַח"ב.

רַבִּי יוֹסֵי הַגְּלִילִי אוֹמֵר: מִנַּיִן אַתָּה אוֹמֵר שֶׁלָּקוּ הַמִּצְרִים בְּמִצְרַיִם עֶשֶׂר מַכּוֹת וְעַל הַיָּם לָקוּ חֲמִשִׁים מַכּוֹת? בְּמִצְרַיִם מַה הוּא אוֹמֵר? וַיֹּאמְרוּ הַחַרְטֻמִּם אֶל פַּרְעֹה: אֶצְבַּע אֱלֹהִים הוּא, וְעַל הַיָּם מָה הוּא אוֹמֵר? וַיַּרְא יִשְׂרָאֵל אֶת-הַיָּד הַגְּדֹלָה אֲשֶׁר עָשָׂה ה' בְּמִצְרַיִם, וַיִּירְאוּ הָעָם אֶת-ה', וַיַּאֲמִינוּ בַּיי וּבְמֹשֶׁה עַבְדּוֹ. כַּמָּה לָקוּ בָאֶצְבַּע? עֶשֶׂר מַכּוֹת. אֱמוֹר מֵעַתָּה: בְּמִצְרַיִם לָקוּ עֶשֶׂר מַכּוֹת וְעַל הַיָּם לָקוּ חֲמִשִׁים מַכּוֹת.

רַבִּי אֱלִיעֶזֶר אוֹמֵר: מִנַּיִן שֶׁכָּל-מַכָּה וּמַכָּה שֶׁהֵבִיא הַקָּדוֹשׁ בָּרוּךְ הוּא עַל הַמִּצְרִים בְּמִצְרַיִם הָיְתָה שֶׁל אַרְבַּע מַכּוֹת? שֶׁנֶּאֱמַר: יְשַׁלַּח-בָּם חֲרוֹן אַפּוֹ, עֶבְרָה וָזַעַם וְצָרָה, מִשְׁלַחַת מַלְאֲכֵי רָעִים. עֶבְרָה - אַחַת, וָזַעַם - שְׁתַּיִם, וְצָרָה - שָׁלֹשׁ, מִשְׁלַחַת מַלְאֲכֵי רָעִים - אַרְבַּע. אֱמוֹר מֵעַתָּה: בְּמִצְרַיִם לָקוּ אַרְבָּעִים מַכּוֹת וְעַל הַיָּם לָקוּ מָאתַיִם מַכּוֹת.

רַבִּי עֲקִיבָא אוֹמֵר: מִנַּיִן שֶׁכָּל-מַכָּה וּמַכָּה שֶׁהֵבִיא הַקָּדוֹשׁ בָּרוּךְ הוּא עַל הַמִּצְרִים בְּמִצְרַיִם הָיְתָה שֶׁל חָמֵשׁ מַכּוֹת? שֶׁנֶּאֱמַר: יְשַׁלַּח-בָּם חֲרוֹן אַפּוֹ, עֶבְרָה וָזַעַם וְצָרָה, מִשְׁלַחַת מַלְאֲכֵי רָעִים. חֲרוֹן אַפּוֹ- אַחַת, עֶבְרָה - שְׁתַּיִם, וָזַעַם - שָׁלוֹשׁ, וְצָרָה - אַרְבַּע, מִשְׁלַחַת מַלְאֲכֵי רָעִים - חָמֵשׁ. אֱמוֹר מֵעַתָּה: בְּמִצְרַיִם לָקוּ חֲמִשִׁים מַכּוֹת וְעַל הַיָּם לָקוּ חֲמִשִׁים וּמָאתַיִם מַכּוֹת.

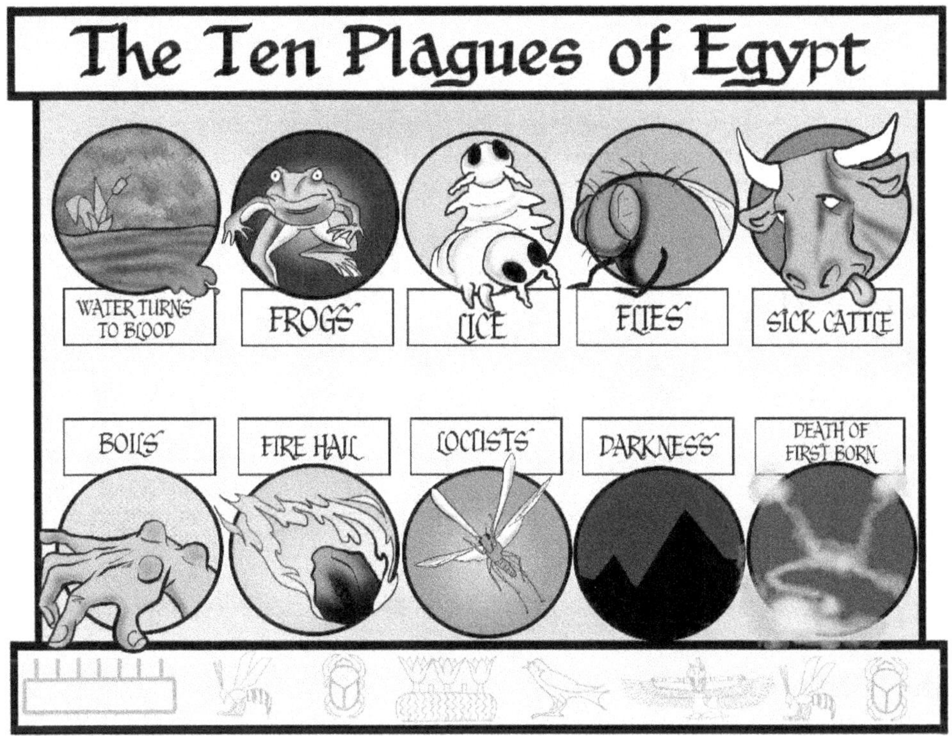

[21]

(Directions: as each plague, the words "blood and fire and pillars of smoke, is mentioned each person at the table places there pinky finger tip into their wines and removes one drop.)

(Culture: this is done to show our sadness that the LORD had to bring the plagues upon Egypt. Only one drop is removed because we are not that sorry.)

Explanation to this part of the Seder: "With a strong hand" [corresponds to] two [plagues]; "and with an outstretched forearm" [corresponds to] two [plagues]; "and with great awe" [corresponds to] two [plagues]; "and with signs" [corresponds to] two [plagues]; "and with wonders" [corresponds to] two [plagues].

---

[21] https://i.pinimg.com/originals/77/06/3e/77063e141772c2b6d11564b0af6f44fb.jpg. Accessed 3/30/2022.

These are [the] ten plagues that the Holy One, blessed be He, brought on the Egyptians in Egypt and they are:

Blood

Frogs

Lice

[The] Mixture [of Wild Animals]

Pestilence

Boils

Hail

Locusts

Darkness

Slaying of [the] Firstborn

Commentary about the Ten Plagues – it can be read as a part of the ritual.

Rabbi Yehuda was accustomed to giving [the plagues] mnemonics: *Detsakh* [the Hebrew initials of the first three plagues], *Adash* [the Hebrew initials of the second three plagues], *Beachav* [the Hebrew initials of the last four plagues].

Rabbi Yose Hagelili said, "From where can you [derive] that the Egyptians were struck with ten plagues in Egypt and struck with fifty plagues at the Sea? In Egypt, what does it state? 'Then the magicians said unto Pharaoh: 'This is the *finger* of God' (Exodus 8:15). And at the Sea, what does it state? 'And Israel saw the Lord's great *hand* that he used upon the Egyptians, and the people feared the Lord; and they believed in the Lord, and in Moshe, His servant' (Exodus 14:31). How many were they struck with with the finger? Ten plagues. You can say from here that in Egypt, they were struck with ten plagues and at the Sea, they were struck with fifty plagues."

Rabbi Eliezer said, "From where [can you derive] that every plague that the Holy One, blessed be He, brought upon the Egyptians in Egypt was [composed] of four plagues? As it is stated (Psalms 78:49): 'He sent upon them the fierceness of His anger, wrath, and fury, and trouble, a sending of messengers of evil.' 'Wrath' [corresponds to] one; 'and fury' [brings it to] two; 'and trouble' [brings it to] three; 'a sending of messengers of evil' [brings it to] four. You can say from here that in Egypt, they were struck with forty plagues and at the Sea, they were struck with two hundred plagues."

Rabbi Akiva said, said, "From where [can you derive] that every plague that the Holy One, blessed be He, brought upon the Egyptians in Egypt was [composed] of five plagues? As it is stated (Psalms 78:49): 'He sent upon them the fierceness of His anger, wrath, and fury, and trouble, a sending of messengers of evil.' 'The fierceness of His anger' [corresponds to] one; 'wrath' [brings it to] two; 'and fury' [brings it to] three; 'and trouble' [brings it to] four; 'a sending of messengers of evil' [brings it to] five. You can say from here that in Egypt, they were struck with fifty plagues and at the Sea, they were struck with two hundred and fifty plagues."

<u>הגדה של פסח, מגיד, דיינו א׳-ט״ז</u>

כַּמָּה מַעֲלוֹת טוֹבוֹת לַמָּקוֹם עָלֵינוּ!

אִלּוּ הוֹצִיאָנוּ מִמִּצְרַיִם וְלֹא עָשָׂה בָהֶם שְׁפָטִים, דַּיֵּנוּ.

אִלּוּ עָשָׂה בָהֶם שְׁפָטִים, וְלֹא עָשָׂה בֵאלֹהֵיהֶם, דַּיֵּנוּ.

אִלּוּ עָשָׂה בֵאלֹהֵיהֶם, וְלֹא הָרַג אֶת-בְּכוֹרֵיהֶם, דַּיֵּנוּ.

אִלּוּ הָרַג אֶת-בְּכוֹרֵיהֶם וְלֹא נָתַן לָנוּ אֶת-מָמוֹנָם, דַּיֵּנוּ.

אִלּוּ נָתַן לָנוּ אֶת-מָמוֹנָם וְלֹא קָרַע לָנוּ אֶת-הַיָּם, דַּיֵּנוּ.

אִלּוּ קָרַע לָנוּ אֶת-הַיָּם וְלֹא הֶעֱבִירָנוּ בְתוֹכוֹ בֶּחָרָבָה, דַּיֵּנוּ.

אִלּוּ הֶעֱבִירָנוּ בְתוֹכוֹ בֶּחָרָבָה וְלֹא שִׁקַּע צָרֵנוּ בְּתוֹכוֹ דַּיֵּנוּ

אִלּוּ שִׁקַּע צָרֵנוּ בְּתוֹכוֹ וְלֹא סִפֵּק צָרְכֵּנוּ בַּמִּדְבָּר אַרְבָּעִים שָׁנָה דַּיֵּנוּ.

אִלּוּ סִפֵּק צָרְכֵּנוּ בַּמִּדְבָּר אַרְבָּעִים שָׁנָה וְלֹא הֶאֱכִילָנוּ אֶת-הַמָּן דַּיֵּנוּ.

אִלּוּ הֶאֱכִילָנוּ אֶת-הַמָּן וְלֹא נָתַן לָנוּ אֶת-הַשַּׁבָּת, דַּיֵּנוּ.

אִלּוּ נָתַן לָנוּ אֶת-הַשַּׁבָּת, וְלֹא קֵרְבָנוּ לִפְנֵי הַר סִינַי, דַּיֵּנוּ.

אִלּוּ קֵרְבָנוּ לִפְנֵי הַר סִינַי, וְלֹא נַתַן לָנוּ אֶת-הַתּוֹרָה. דַּיֵּנוּ.

אִלּוּ נַתַן לָנוּ אֶת-הַתּוֹרָה וְלֹא הִכְנִיסָנוּ לְאֶרֶץ יִשְׂרָאֵל, דַּיֵּנוּ.

אִלּוּ הִכְנִיסָנוּ לְאֶרֶץ יִשְׂרָאֵל וְלֹא בָנָה לָנוּ אֶת-בֵּית הַבְּחִירָה דַּיֵּנוּ.

עַל אַחַת, כַּמָּה וְכַמָּה, טוֹבָה כְפוּלָה וּמְכֻפֶּלֶת לַמָּקוֹם עָלֵינוּ: שֶׁהוֹצִיאָנוּ מִמִּצְרַיִם, וְעָשָׂה בָהֶם שְׁפָטִים וְעָשָׂה בֵאלֹהֵיהֶם, וְהָרַג אֶת-בְּכוֹרֵיהֶם, וְנָתַן לָנוּ אֶת-מָמוֹנָם, וְקָרַע לָנוּ אֶת-הַיָּם, וְהֶעֱבִירָנוּ בְתוֹכוֹ בֶּחָרָבָה, וְשִׁקַּע צָרֵנוּ בְּתוֹכוֹ, וְסִפֵּק צָרְכֵּנוּ בַּמִּדְבָּר אַרְבָּעִים שָׁנָה, וְהֶאֱכִילָנוּ אֶת-הַמָּן, וְנָתַן לָנוּ אֶת-הַשַּׁבָּת, וְקֵרְבָנוּ לִפְנֵי הַר סִינַי, וְנָתַן לָנוּ אֶת-הַתּוֹרָה, וְהִכְנִיסָנוּ לְאֶרֶץ יִשְׂרָאֵל, וּבָנָה לָנוּ אֶת-בֵּית הַבְּחִירָה לְכַפֵּר עַל-כָּל-עֲוֹנוֹתֵינוּ.

Dreams

(Usually read in unison – however it can be recited anyone the group wishes)

How many degrees of good did the Place [of all bestow] upon us!

If He had taken us out of Egypt and not made judgements on them; [it would have been] enough for us.

If He had made judgments on them and had not made [them] on their gods; [it would have been] enough for us.

If He had made [them] on their gods and had not killed their firstborn; [it would have been] enough for us.

If He had killed their firstborn and had not given us their money; [it would have been] enough for us.

If He had given us their money and had not split the Sea for us; [it would have been] enough for us.

If He had split the Sea for us and had not taken us through it on dry land; [it would have been] enough for us.

If He had taken us through it on dry land and had not pushed down our enemies in [the Sea]; [it would have been] enough for us.

---

22 https://trendpickle.com/wp-content/uploads/2018/07/realm-of-dreams-4.jpg. Accessed 3/30/2022.

If He had pushed down our enemies in [the Sea] and had not supplied our needs in the wilderness for forty years; [it would have been] enough for us.

If He had supplied our needs in the wilderness for forty years and had not fed us the manna; [it would have been] enough for us.

If He had fed us the manna and had not given us the Shabbat; [it would have been] enough for us.

If He had given us the Shabbat and had not brought us close to Mount Sinai; [it would have been] enough for us.

If He had brought us close to Mount Sinai and had not given us the Torah; [it would have been] enough for us.

If He had given us the Torah and had not brought us into the land of Israel; [it would have been] enough for us.

If He had brought us into the land of Israel and had not built us the 'Chosen House' [the Temple; it would have been] enough for us.

How much more so is the good that is doubled and quadrupled that the Place [of all bestowed] upon us [enough for us]; since he took us out of Egypt, and made judgments with them, and made [them] with their gods, and killed their firstborn, and gave us their money, and split the Sea for us, and brought us through it on dry land, and pushed down our enemies in [the Sea], and supplied our needs in the wilderness for forty years, and fed us the manna, and gave us the Shabbat, and brought us close to Mount Sinai, and gave us the Torah, and brought us into the land of Israel and built us the 'Chosen House' [the Temple] to atone upon all of our sins.

<u>הגדה של פסח ,מגיד ,פסח מצה ומרור א'-ז'</u>
רַבָּן גַּמְלִיאֵל הָיָה אוֹמֵר :כָּל שֶׁלֹּא אָמַר שְׁלשָׁה דְּבָרִים אֵלּוּ בַּפֶּסַח ,לֹא יָצָא יְדֵי חוֹבָתוֹ ,וְאֵלּוּ הֵן :פֶּסַח ,מַצָּה ,וּמָרוֹר.
פֶּסַח שֶׁהָיוּ אֲבוֹתֵינוּ אוֹכְלִים בִּזְמַן שֶׁבֵּית הַמִּקְדָּשׁ הָיָה קַיָּם ,עַל שׁוּם מָה ?עַל שׁוּם שֶׁפָּסַח הַקָּדוֹשׁ בָּרוּךְ הוּא עַל בָּתֵּי אֲבוֹתֵינוּ בְּמִצְרַיִם ,שֶׁנֶּאֱמַר :וַאֲמַרְתֶּם זֶבַח פֶּסַח הוּא לַיי ,אֲשֶׁר פָּסַח עַל בָּתֵּי בְנֵי יִשְׂרָאֵל בְּמִצְרַיִם בְּנָגְפּוֹ אֶת-מִצְרַיִם ,וְאֶת-בָּתֵּינוּ הִצִּיל ?וַיִּקֹּד הָעָם וַיִּשְׁתַּחֲווּ.
אוחז המצה בידו ומראה אותה למסובין:

70

מַצָּה זוֹ שֶׁאָנוּ אוֹכְלִים, עַל שׁוּם מַה? עַל שׁוּם שֶׁלֹּא הִסְפִּיק בְּצֵקָם שֶׁל אֲבוֹתֵינוּ לְהַחֲמִיץ עַד שֶׁנִּגְלָה
עֲלֵיהֶם מֶלֶךְ מַלְכֵי הַמְּלָכִים, הַקָּדוֹשׁ בָּרוּךְ הוּא, וּגְאָלָם, שֶׁנֶּאֱמַר: וַיֹּאפוּ אֶת-הַבָּצֵק אֲשֶׁר הוֹצִיאוּ מִמִּצְרַיִם
עֻגֹת מַצּוֹת, כִּי לֹא חָמֵץ, כִּי גֹרְשׁוּ מִמִּצְרַיִם וְלֹא יָכְלוּ לְהִתְמַהְמֵהַּ, וְגַם צֵדָה לֹא עָשׂוּ לָהֶם.

אוחז המרור בידו ומראה אותו למסובין:

מָרוֹר זֶה שֶׁאָנוּ אוֹכְלִים, עַל שׁוּם מַה? עַל שׁוּם שֶׁמֵּרְרוּ הַמִּצְרִים אֶת-חַיֵּי אֲבוֹתֵינוּ בְּמִצְרַיִם, שֶׁנֶּאֱמַר:
וַיְמָרְרוּ אֶת חַיֵּיהֶם בַּעֲבֹדָה קָשָׁה, בְּחֹמֶר וּבִלְבֵנִים וּבְכָל-עֲבֹדָה בַּשָּׂדֶה אֵת כָּל-עֲבֹדָתָם אֲשֶׁר עָבְדוּ בָהֶם
בְּפָרֶךְ.

בְּכָל-דּוֹר וָדוֹר חַיָּב אָדָם לִרְאוֹת אֶת-עַצְמוֹ כְּאִלּוּ הוּא יָצָא מִמִּצְרַיִם, שֶׁנֶּאֱמַר: וְהִגַּדְתָּ לְבִנְךָ בַּיּוֹם הַהוּא
לֵאמֹר, בַּעֲבוּר זֶה עָשָׂה ה' לִי בְּצֵאתִי מִמִּצְרָיִם. לֹא אֶת-אֲבוֹתֵינוּ בִּלְבָד גָּאַל הַקָּדוֹשׁ בָּרוּךְ הוּא, אֶלָּא אַף
אוֹתָנוּ גָּאַל עִמָּהֶם, שֶׁנֶּאֱמַר: וְאוֹתָנוּ הוֹצִיא מִשָּׁם, לְמַעַן הָבִיא אוֹתָנוּ, לָתֶת לָנוּ אֶת-הָאָרֶץ אֲשֶׁר נִשְׁבַּע
לַאֲבֹתֵינוּ.

Rabban Gamiliel's Three Things

(This can be a shared reading around the Seder table)

Rabban Gamliel was accustomed to say, Anyone who has not said these three things on Pesach has not fulfilled his obligation, and these are them: the Pesach sacrifice, matzah and *marror.*

The Pesach [passover] sacrifice that our ancestors were accustomed to eating when the Temple existed, for the sake of what [was it]? For the sake [to commemorate] that the Holy One, blessed be He, passed over the homes of our ancestors in Egypt, as it is stated (Exodus 12:27); "And you shall say: 'It is the passover sacrifice to the Lord, for that He passed over the homes of the Children of Israel in Egypt, when He smote the Egyptians, and our homes he saved.' And the people bowed the head and bowed." He holds the matzah in his hand and shows it to the others there.

---

23 https://live.staticflickr.com/4907/47389943311_a45b34b07e.jpg. Accessed 3/30/2022.

This matzah that we are eating, for the sake of what [is it]? For the sake [to commemorate] that our ancestors' dough was not yet able to rise, before the King of the kings of kings, the Holy One, blessed be He, revealed [Himself] to them and redeemed them, as it is stated (Exodus 12:39); "And they baked the dough which they brought out of Egypt into matzah cakes, since it did not rise; because they were expelled from Egypt, and could not tarry, neither had they made for themselves provisions."
He holds the marror in his hand and shows it to the others there.

This marror [bitter greens] that we are eating, for the sake of what [is it]? For the sake [to commemorate] that the Egyptians embittered the lives of our ancestors in Egypt, as it is stated (Exodus 1:14); "And they made their lives bitter with hard service, in mortar and in brick, and in all manner of service in the field; in all their service, wherein they made them serve with rigor."

In each and every generation, a person is obligated to see himself as if he left Egypt, as it is stated (Exodus 13:8); "For the sake of this, did the Lord do [this] for me in *my* going out of Egypt." Not only our ancestors did the Holy One, blessed be He, redeem, but rather also us [together] with them did he redeem, as it is stated (Deuteronomy 6:23); "And He took us out from there, in order to bring us in, to give us the land which He swore unto our fathers."

<u>הגדה של פסח ,מגיד ,חצי הלל א'-ד'</u>
יאחז הכוס בידו ויכסה המצות ויאמר:
לְפִיכָךְ אֲנַחְנוּ חַיָּבִים לְהוֹדוֹת ,לְהַלֵּל ,לְשַׁבֵּחַ ,לְפָאֵר ,לְרוֹמֵם ,לְהַדֵּר ,לְבָרֵךְ ,לְעַלֵּה וּלְקַלֵּס לְמִי שֶׁעָשָׂה לַאֲבוֹתֵינוּ וְלָנוּ אֶת-כָּל-הַנִּסִּים הָאֵלּוּ: הוֹצִיאָנוּ מֵעַבְדוּת לְחֵרוּת מִיָּגוֹן לְשִׂמְחָה ,וּמֵאֵבֶל לְיוֹם טוֹב ,וּמֵאֲפֵלָה לְאוֹר גָּדוֹל ,וּמִשִּׁעְבּוּד לִגְאֻלָּה .וְנֹאמַר לְפָנָיו שִׁירָה חֲדָשָׁה :הַלְלוּיָהּ.
הַלְלוּיָהּ הַלְלוּ עַבְדֵי ה ,'הַלְלוּ אֶת-שֵׁם ה .'יְהִי שֵׁם ה 'מְבֹרָךְ מֵעַתָּה וְעַד עוֹלָם .מִמִּזְרַח שֶׁמֶשׁ עַד מְבוֹאוֹ מְהֻלָּל שֵׁם ה .'רָם עַל-כָּל-גּוֹיִם ה ,'עַל הַשָּׁמַיִם כְּבוֹדוֹ.מִי כַּיי אֱלֹהֵינוּ הַמַּגְבִּיהִי לָשָׁבֶת ,הַמַּשְׁפִּילִי לִרְאוֹת בַּשָּׁמַיִם וּבָאָרֶץ? מְקִימִי מֵעָפָר דָּל ,מֵאַשְׁפֹּת יָרִים אֶבְיוֹן ,לְהוֹשִׁיבִי עִם-נְדִיבִים ,עִם נְדִיבֵי עַמּוֹ .מוֹשִׁיבִי עֲקֶרֶת הַבַּיִת ,אֵם הַבָּנִים שְׂמֵחָה .הַלְלוּיָהּ.

בְּצֵאת יִשְׂרָאֵל מִמִּצְרָיִם, בֵּית יַעֲקֹב מֵעַם לֹעֵז, הָיְתָה יְהוּדָה לְקָדְשׁוֹ, יִשְׂרָאֵל מַמְשְׁלוֹתָיו. הַיָּם רָאָה וַיָּנֹס,
הַיַּרְדֵּן יִסֹּב לְאָחוֹר. הֶהָרִים רָקְדוּ כְאֵילִים, גְּבָעוֹת כִּבְנֵי צֹאן. מַה לְּךָ הַיָּם כִּי תָנוּס, הַיַּרְדֵּן - תִּסֹּב לְאָחוֹר.
הֶהָרִים - תִּרְקְדוּ כְאֵילִים, גְּבָעוֹת כִּבְנֵי-צֹאן. מִלְּפָנֵי אָדוֹן חוּלִי אָרֶץ, מִלְּפָנֵי אֱלוֹהַּ יַעֲקֹב. הַהֹפְכִי הַצּוּר
אֲגַם-מָיִם, חַלָּמִישׁ לְמַעְיְנוֹ-מָיִם.

First Half of the Hallel

Definition: HALLEL (Heb. הַלֵּל), the general term designating Psalms 113–118 when these form a unit in the liturgy. These psalms are essentially expressions of thanksgiving and joy for divine redemption. Hallel is recited in two forms: (a) The "full" Hallel, consisting of Psalms 113–118. It is chanted in the synagogue on Sukkot , Ḥanukkah , the first day of Passover (the first two days in the Diaspora), Shavu'Ot , and (in many synagogues) Israel Independence Day. Hallel is also recited during the Passover seder service, when it is known as Hallel Miẓri ("Egyptian Hallel") because of the exodus from Egypt which the seder commemorates.

(Directions: The leader holds the cup in his hand and covers the matzah and says.)

Therefore, we are obligated to thank, praise, laud, glorify, exalt, lavish, bless, raise high, and acclaim He who made all these miracles for our ancestors and for us: He brought us out from slavery to freedom, from sorrow to joy, from mourning to [celebration of]

---

[24] https://www.ou.org/holidays/files/Hallel-e1462941372473.jpg. Accessed 3/30/2022.

a festival, from darkness to great light, and from servitude to redemption. And let us say a new song before Him, Halleluyah!

Halleluyah! Praise, servants of the Lord, praise the name of the Lord. May the Name of the Lord be blessed from now and forever. From the rising of the sun in the East to its setting, the name of the Lord is praised. Above all nations is the Lord, His honor is above the heavens. Who is like the Lord, our God, Who sits on high; Who looks down upon the heavens and the earth? He brings up the poor out of the dirt; from the refuse piles, He raises the destitute. To seat him with the nobles, with the nobles of his people. He seats a barren woman in a home, a happy mother of children. Halleluyah! (Psalms 113)

In Israel's going out from Egypt, the house of Ya'akov from a people of foreign speech. The Sea saw and fled, the Jordan turned to the rear. The mountains danced like rams, the hills like young sheep. What is happening to you, O Sea, that you are fleeing, O Jordan that you turn to the rear; O mountains that you dance like rams, O hills like young sheep? From before the Master, tremble O earth, from before the Lord of Ya'akov. He who turns the boulder into a pond of water, the flint into a spring of water. (Psalms 114)

<u>הגדה של פסח, מגיד, כוס שניה א'-ד'</u>
מגביהים את הכוס עד גאל ישראל.
בָּרוּךְ אַתָּה ה' אֱלֹהֵינוּ מֶלֶךְ הָעוֹלָם, אֲשֶׁר גְּאָלָנוּ וְגָאַל אֶת-אֲבוֹתֵינוּ מִמִּצְרַיִם, וְהִגִּיעָנוּ הַלַּיְלָה הַזֶּה לֶאֱכָל-
בּוֹ מַצָּה וּמָרוֹר. כֵּן ה' אֱלֹהֵינוּ וֵאלֹהֵי אֲבוֹתֵינוּ יַגִּיעֵנוּ לְמוֹעֲדִים וְלִרְגָלִים אֲחֵרִים הַבָּאִים לִקְרָאתֵנוּ לְשָׁלוֹם,
שְׂמֵחִים בְּבִנְיַן עִירֶךָ וְשָׂשִׂים בַּעֲבוֹדָתֶךָ. וְנֹאכַל שָׁם מִן הַזְּבָחִים וּמִן הַפְּסָחִים אֲשֶׁר יַגִּיעַ דָּמָם עַל קִיר
מִזְבַּחֲךָ לְרָצוֹן, וְנוֹדֶה לְךָ שִׁיר חָדָשׁ עַל גְּאֻלָּתֵנוּ וְעַל פְּדוּת נַפְשֵׁנוּ. בָּרוּךְ אַתָּה ה', גָּאַל יִשְׂרָאֵל.
שותים את הכוס בהסבת שמאל.
בָּרוּךְ אַתָּה ה', אֱלֹהֵינוּ מֶלֶךְ הָעוֹלָם בּוֹרֵא פְּרִי הַגָּפֶן.

Second Cup of Wine

Why four cups of wine by the seder?[26]

Wine is considered a royal drink, one that symbolizes freedom. It is the appropriate beverage for the nights when we celebrate our freedom from Egyptian bondage. Many reasons are given for drinking four cups of wine. Here are some of them:

When promised to deliver the Jews from Egyptian slavery, G-d used four terms to describe the redemption (Exodus 6:6-8): a) "I shall take you out..." b) "I shall rescue you..." c) "I shall redeem you..." d) "I shall bring you..."

The four cups symbolize our freedom from our four exiles. We were liberated from Pharaoh's four evil decrees: a) Slavery. b) The ordered murder of all male progeny by the Hebrew midwives. c) The drowning of all Hebrew boys in the Nile by Egyptian thugs. d) The decree ordering the Israelites to collect their own straw for use in their brick production.

---

[25] http://messiahinthepassover.com. Accessed 3/30/2022.

[26] https://www.chabad.org/holidays/passover/pesach_cdo/aid/658549/jewish/Why-four-cups-of-wine.htm. Accessed 3/30/2022.

The four cups symbolize our freedom from our <u>four exiles</u>: The Egyptian, Babylonian, and Greek exiles, and our current exile which we hope to be rid of very soon with the coming of Moshiach.

The words "cup of wine" are mentioned four times in Pharaoh's butler's dream (<u>Genesis 40:11</u>-13). According to the Midrash, these cups of wine alluded to the Israelites' liberation.

According to Kabbalah, there are four forces of impurity (anti-divinity, or kelipah). On Passover, when we celebrate our physical freedom, we also celebrate our liberation from these spiritual forces. Our physical departure from Egypt was a reflection of our spiritual one—we were pulled from the clutches of depravity and impurity and set on the path to receiving the Torah and connecting with God.

(Direction: Raise cups)

We raise the cup until we reach "who redeemed Israel"

Blessed are You, Lord our God, King of the universe, who redeemed us and redeemed our ancestors from Egypt, and brought us on this night to eat matzah and *marror*, so too, Lord our God, and God of our ancestors, bring us to other appointed times and holidays that will come to greet us in peace, joyful in the building of your city and happy in your worship; that we should eat there from the offerings and from the Pesach sacrifices, the blood of which should reach the wall of your altar for favor, and we shall thank you with a new song upon our redemption and upon the restoration of our souls. Blessed are you, Lord, who redeemed Israel.

We say the blessing below and drink the cup while reclining to the left

Blessed are You, Lord our God, who creates the fruit of the vine.

<u>הגדה של פסח ,רחצה א׳-ג׳</u>

רָחְצָה

נוטלים את הידים ומברכים:

בָּרוּךְ אַתָּה ה׳, אֱלֹהֵינוּ מֶלֶךְ הָעוֹלָם, אֲשֶׁר קִדְּשָׁנוּ בְּמִצְוֹתָיו וְצִוָּנוּ עַל נְטִילַת יָדַיִם.

Rachtzah – Washing the hands

Blessed are You, Lord our God, King of the Universe, who has sanctified us with His commandments and has commanded us on the washing of the hands.

הגדה של פסח ,מוציא מצה א'-ד'

מוֹצִיא מַצָּה

יקח המצות בסדר שהניחן ,הפרוסה בין שתי השלמות ,יאחז שלשתן בידו ויברך "המוציא "בכוונה עַל העליונה ,ו"על אכילת מַצָּה "בכוונה על הפרוסה .אחר כך יבצע כזית מן העליונה השלמה וכזית שני מן הפרוסה ,ויטבלם במלח ,ויאכל בהסה שני הזיתים:

בָּרוּךְ אַתָּה ה ,'אֱלֹהֵינוּ מֶלֶךְ הָעוֹלָם הַמּוֹצִיא לֶחֶם מִן הָאָרֶץ.

בָּרוּךְ אַתָּה ה ,'אֱלֹהֵינוּ מֶלֶךְ הָעוֹלָם ,אֲשֶׁר קִדְּשָׁנוּ בְּמִצְוֹתָיו וְצִוָּנוּ עַל אֲכִילַת מַצָּה.

---

[27] http://haggadot.com. Accessed 3/30/2022.

Motzi Matzah

(Directions: The leader takes out the matzah in the order that he placed them, the broken one between the two whole ones; he holds the three of them in his hand and blesses "ha-motsi" with the intention to take from the top one and "on eating matzah" with the intention of eating from the broken one. Afterwards, he breaks off a kazayit from the top whole one and a second kazayit from the broken one and he dips them into salt and eats both while reclining.)

Blessed are You, Lord our God, King of the Universe, who brings forth bread from the ground.

Blessed are You, Lord our God, King of the Universe, who has sanctified us with His commandments and has commanded us on the eating of matzah.

<u>הגדה של פסח, מרור א'-ג'</u>

מָרוֹר

כל אחד מהמסבים לוקח כזית מרור, מטבלו בַחרוסת, מנער החרוסת, מברך ואוכל בלי הסבה.

בָּרוּךְ אַתָּה ה', אֱלֹהֵינוּ מֶלֶךְ הָעוֹלָם, אֲשֶׁר קִדְּשָׁנוּ בְּמִצְוֹתָיו וְצִוָּנוּ עַל אֲכִילַת מָרוֹר.

Marror

29

(Directions: All present should take a kazayit of marror, dip into the haroset, shake off the haroset, make the blessing and eat without reclining.)

Blessed are You, Lord our God, King of the Universe, who has sanctified us with His commandments and has commanded us on the eating of marror.

<u>הגדה של פסח ,כורך א'-ד'</u>

כּוֹרֵךְ

כל אחד מהמסבים לוקח כזית מן המצה השְּׁלישית עם כזית מרור,כורכים יחד ,אוכלים בהסבה ובלי ברכה. לפני אכלו אומר

זֵכֶר לְמִקְדָּשׁ כְּהִלֵּל .כֵּן עָשָׂה הִלֵּל בִּזְמַן שֶׁבֵּית הַמִּקְדָּשׁ הָיָה קַיָּם:

הָיָה כּוֹרֵךְ מַצָּה וּמָרוֹר וְאוֹכֵל בְּיַחַד ,לְקַיֵּם מַה שֶּׁנֶּאֱמַר :עַל מַצּוֹת וּמְרוֹרִים יֹאכְלֻהוּ.

---

[29] http://elanaspantry.com. Accessed 3/30/2022.

Korech – Wrap

(*Directions: All present should take a kazayit from the third whole matzah with a kazayit of marror, wrap them together and eat them while reclining and without saying a blessing. Before the leader eats it, he should say.*)

In memory of the Temple according to Hillel. This is what Hillel would do when the Temple existed:

(*Directions: The leader wraps the matzah and marror and eat them together, in order to fulfill what is stated, (Exodus 12:15)):*)

"You should eat it upon Matzot and marrorim."

הגדה של פסח ,שולחן עורך א׳-ב׳

שֻׁלְחָן עוֹרֵךְ

.אוכלים ושותים

---

[30] http://oukosher.com. Accessed 3/30/2022.

Meal

(Directions: eat the meal)

We eat and drink.

<u>הגדה של פסח ,צפון א'-ג'</u>

צָפוּן

אחר גמר הסעודה לוקח כל אחד מהמסבים כזית מהמצה שהייתה צפונה לאפיקומן ואוכל ממנה כזית
בהסבה .וצריך לאוכלה קודם חצות הלילה.

לפני אכילת האפיקומן יאמר :זֵכֶר לְקָרְבָּן פֶּסַח הַנֶּאֱכָל עַל הַשּׂוֹבַע.

---

[31] http://forward.com. Accessed 3/30/2022.

Tzafun - The Concealed [Matzah]

(Directions: After the end of the meal, all those present take a kazayit from the matzah, that was concealed for the afikoman, and eat a kazayit from it while reclining. Before eating the afikoman, he should say).

(Culture: Usually, the child finding it gets a dollar bill or any denomination the leader wants to give. Usually, all the children get money.)

In memory of the Pesach sacrifice that was eaten upon being satiated.

<u>הגדה של פסח ,ברך ,ברכת המזון א'-כ״ג</u>

בָּרֵךְ

מוזגים כוס שלישי ומברכים ברכת המזון.

שִׁיר הַמַּעֲלוֹת ,בְּשׁוּב ה 'אֶת שִׁיבַת צִיּוֹן הָיִינוּ כְּחֹלְמִים .אָז יִמָּלֵא שְׂחוֹק פִּינוּ וּלְשׁוֹנֵנוּ רִנָּה .אָז יֹאמְרוּ בַגּוֹיִם :הִגְדִּיל ה 'לַעֲשׂוֹת עִם אֵלֶּה .הִגְדִּיל ה 'לַעֲשׂוֹת עִמָּנוּ ,הָיִינוּ שְׂמֵחִים .שׁוּבָה ה 'אֶת שְׁבִיתֵנוּ כַּאֲפִיקִים בַּנֶּגֶב .הַזֹּרְעִים בְּדִמְעָה ,בְּרִנָּה יִקְצֹרוּ .הָלוֹךְ יֵלֵךְ וּבָכֹה נֹשֵׂא מֶשֶׁךְ הַזָּרַע ,בֹּא יָבֹא בְרִנָּה נֹשֵׂא אֲלֻמֹּתָיו.

שלשה שֶׁאכלו כאחד חיבים לזמן והמזַמן פותח:

רַבּוֹתַי נְבָרֵךְ:

המסבים עונים:

יְהִי שֵׁם ה 'מְבֹרָךְ מֵעַתָּה וְעַד עוֹלָם.

הַמְזַמֵּן אוֹמֵר:

בִּרְשׁוּת מָרָנָן וְרַבָּנָן וְרַבּוֹתַי ,נְבָרֵךְ] אֱלֹהֵינוּ [שֶׁאָכַלְנוּ מִשֶּׁלוֹ.

המסבים עונים:

בָּרוּךְ] אֱלֹהֵינוּ [שֶׁאָכַלְנוּ מִשֶּׁלוֹ וּבְטוּבוֹ חָיִינוּ

המזמן חוזר ואומר:

בָּרוּךְ] אֱלֹהֵינוּ [שֶׁאָכַלְנוּ מִשֶּׁלוֹ וּבְטוּבוֹ חָיִינוּ

---

[32] https://w3.chabad.org/media/images/126/wKwg1261849.jpg. Accessed 3/30/2022.

כלם אומרים:
בָּרוּךְ אַתָּה ה', אֱלֹהֵינוּ מֶלֶךְ הָעוֹלָם, הַזָּן אֶת הָעוֹלָם כֻּלּוֹ בְּטוּבוֹ בְּחֵן בְּחֶסֶד וּבְרַחֲמִים, הוּא נוֹתֵן לֶחֶם לְכָל בָּשָׂר כִּי לְעוֹלָם חַסְדּוֹ. וּבְטוּבוֹ הַגָּדוֹל תָּמִיד לֹא חָסַר לָנוּ, וְאַל יֶחְסַר לָנוּ מָזוֹן לְעוֹלָם וָעֶד. בַּעֲבוּר שְׁמוֹ הַגָּדוֹל, כִּי הוּא אֵל זָן וּמְפַרְנֵס לַכֹּל וּמֵטִיב לַכֹּל, וּמֵכִין מָזוֹן לְכָל בְּרִיּוֹתָיו אֲשֶׁר בָּרָא. בָּרוּךְ אַתָּה ה', הַזָּן אֶת הַכֹּל.

נוֹדֶה לְךָ ה' אֱלֹהֵינוּ עַל שֶׁהִנְחַלְתָּ לַאֲבוֹתֵינוּ אֶרֶץ חֶמְדָּה טוֹבָה וּרְחָבָה, וְעַל שֶׁהוֹצֵאתָנוּ ה' אֱלֹהֵינוּ מֵאֶרֶץ מִצְרַיִם, וּפְדִיתָנוּ מִבֵּית עֲבָדִים, וְעַל בְּרִיתְךָ שֶׁחָתַמְתָּ בִּבְשָׂרֵנוּ, וְעַל תּוֹרָתְךָ שֶׁלִּמַּדְתָּנוּ, וְעַל חֻקֶּיךָ שֶׁהוֹדַעְתָּנוּ, וְעַל חַיִּים חֵן וָחֶסֶד שֶׁחוֹנַנְתָּנוּ, וְעַל אֲכִילַת מָזוֹן שָׁאַתָּה זָן וּמְפַרְנֵס אוֹתָנוּ תָּמִיד, בְּכָל יוֹם וּבְכָל עֵת וּבְכָל שָׁעָה:

וְעַל הַכֹּל ה' אֱלֹהֵינוּ, אֲנַחְנוּ מוֹדִים לָךְ וּמְבָרְכִים אוֹתָךְ, יִתְבָּרַךְ שִׁמְךָ בְּפִי כָּל חַי תָּמִיד לְעוֹלָם וָעֶד. כַּכָּתוּב: וְאָכַלְתָּ וְשָׂבָעְתָּ וּבֵרַכְתָּ אֶת ה' אֱלֹהֶיךָ עַל הָאָרֶץ הַטּוֹבָה אֲשֶׁר נָתַן לָךְ. בָּרוּךְ אַתָּה ה', עַל הָאָרֶץ וְעַל הַמָּזוֹן:

רַחֵם נָא ה' אֱלֹהֵינוּ עַל יִשְׂרָאֵל עַמֶּךָ וְעַל יְרוּשָׁלַיִם עִירֶךָ וְעַל צִיּוֹן מִשְׁכַּן כְּבוֹדֶךָ וְעַל מַלְכוּת בֵּית דָּוִד מְשִׁיחֶךָ וְעַל הַבַּיִת הַגָּדוֹל וְהַקָּדוֹשׁ שֶׁנִּקְרָא שִׁמְךָ עָלָיו: אֱלֹהֵינוּ אָבִינוּ, רְעֵנוּ זוּנֵנוּ פַּרְנְסֵנוּ וְכַלְכְּלֵנוּ וְהַרְוִיחֵנוּ, וְהַרְוַח לָנוּ ה' אֱלֹהֵינוּ מְהֵרָה מִכָּל צָרוֹתֵינוּ. וְנָא אַל תַּצְרִיכֵנוּ ה' אֱלֹהֵינוּ, לֹא לִידֵי מַתְּנַת בָּשָׂר וָדָם וְלֹא לִידֵי הַלְוָאָתָם, כִּי אִם לְיָדְךָ הַמְּלֵאָה הַפְּתוּחָה הַקְּדוֹשָׁה וְהָרְחָבָה, שֶׁלֹּא נֵבוֹשׁ וְלֹא נִכָּלֵם לְעוֹלָם וָעֶד.

בשבת מוסיפין:
רְצֵה וְהַחֲלִיצֵנוּ ה' אֱלֹהֵינוּ בְּמִצְוֹתֶיךָ וּבְמִצְוַת יוֹם הַשְּׁבִיעִי הַשַּׁבָּת הַגָּדוֹל וְהַקָּדוֹשׁ הַזֶּה. כִּי יוֹם זֶה גָּדוֹל וְקָדוֹשׁ הוּא לְפָנֶיךָ לִשְׁבָּת בּוֹ וְלָנוּחַ בּוֹ בְּאַהֲבָה כְּמִצְוַת רְצוֹנֶךָ. וּבִרְצוֹנְךָ הָנִיחַ לָנוּ ה' אֱלֹהֵינוּ שֶׁלֹּא תְהֵא צָרָה וְיָגוֹן וַאֲנָחָה בְּיוֹם מְנוּחָתֵנוּ. וְהַרְאֵנוּ ה' אֱלֹהֵינוּ בְּנֶחָמַת צִיּוֹן עִירֶךָ וּבְבִנְיַן יְרוּשָׁלַיִם עִיר קָדְשֶׁךָ כִּי אַתָּה הוּא בַּעַל הַיְשׁוּעוֹת וּבַעַל הַנֶּחָמוֹת.

אֱלֹהֵינוּ וֵאלֹהֵי אֲבוֹתֵינוּ, יַעֲלֶה וְיָבֹא וְיַגִּיעַ וְיֵרָאֶה וְיֵרָצֶה וְיִשָּׁמַע וְיִפָּקֵד וְיִזָּכֵר זִכְרוֹנֵנוּ וּפִקְדוֹנֵנוּ, וְזִכְרוֹן אֲבוֹתֵינוּ, וְזִכְרוֹן מָשִׁיחַ בֶּן דָּוִד עַבְדֶּךָ, וְזִכְרוֹן יְרוּשָׁלַיִם עִיר קָדְשֶׁךָ, וְזִכְרוֹן כָּל עַמְּךָ בֵּית יִשְׂרָאֵל לְפָנֶיךָ, לִפְלֵיטָה לְטוֹבָה לְחֵן וּלְחֶסֶד וּלְרַחֲמִים, לְחַיִּים וּלְשָׁלוֹם בְּיוֹם חַג הַמַּצּוֹת הַזֶּה זָכְרֵנוּ ה' אֱלֹהֵינוּ בּוֹ לְטוֹבָה וּפָקְדֵנוּ בוֹ לִבְרָכָה וְהוֹשִׁיעֵנוּ בוֹ לְחַיִּים. וּבִדְבַר יְשׁוּעָה וְרַחֲמִים חוּס וְחָנֵּנוּ וְרַחֵם עָלֵינוּ וְהוֹשִׁיעֵנוּ, כִּי אֵלֶיךָ עֵינֵינוּ, כִּי אֵל מֶלֶךְ חַנּוּן וְרַחוּם אָתָּה. וּבְנֵה יְרוּשָׁלַיִם עִיר הַקֹּדֶשׁ בִּמְהֵרָה בְיָמֵינוּ. בָּרוּךְ אַתָּה ה', בּוֹנֵה בְרַחֲמָיו יְרוּשָׁלַיִם. אָמֵן.

בָּרוּךְ אַתָּה ה', אֱלֹהֵינוּ מֶלֶךְ הָעוֹלָם, הָאֵל אָבִינוּ מַלְכֵּנוּ אַדִּירֵנוּ בּוֹרְאֵנוּ גּוֹאֲלֵנוּ יוֹצְרֵנוּ קְדוֹשֵׁנוּ קְדוֹשׁ יַעֲקֹב רוֹעֵנוּ רוֹעֵה יִשְׂרָאֵל הַמֶּלֶךְ הַטּוֹב וְהַמֵּטִיב לַכֹּל שֶׁבְּכָל יוֹם וָיוֹם הוּא הֵטִיב, הוּא מֵטִיב, הוּא יֵיטִיב לָנוּ. הוּא גְמָלָנוּ הוּא גוֹמְלֵנוּ הוּא יִגְמְלֵנוּ לָעַד, לְחֵן וּלְחֶסֶד וּלְרַחֲמִים וּלְרֶוַח הַצָּלָה וְהַצְלָחָה, בְּרָכָה וִישׁוּעָה נֶחָמָה פַּרְנָסָה וְכַלְכָּלָה וְרַחֲמִים וְחַיִּים וְשָׁלוֹם וְכָל טוֹב, וּמִכָּל טוּב לְעוֹלָם עַל יְחַסְּרֵנוּ.

הָרַחֲמָן הוּא יִמְלֹךְ עָלֵינוּ לְעוֹלָם וָעֶד. הָרַחֲמָן הוּא יִתְבָּרַךְ בַּשָּׁמַיִם וּבָאָרֶץ. הָרַחֲמָן הוּא יִשְׁתַּבַּח לְדוֹר דּוֹרִים, וְיִתְפָּאַר בָּנוּ לָעַד וּלְנֵצַח נְצָחִים, וְיִתְהַדַּר בָּנוּ לָעַד וּלְעוֹלְמֵי עוֹלָמִים. הָרַחֲמָן הוּא יְפַרְנְסֵנוּ בְּכָבוֹד. הָרַחֲמָן הוּא יִשְׁבּוֹר עֻלֵּנוּ מֵעַל צַוָּארֵנוּ, וְהוּא יוֹלִיכֵנוּ קוֹמְמִיּוּת לְאַרְצֵנוּ. הָרַחֲמָן הוּא יִשְׁלַח לָנוּ בְּרָכָה מְרֻבָּה בַּבַּיִת הַזֶּה, וְעַל שֻׁלְחָן זֶה שֶׁאָכַלְנוּ עָלָיו. הָרַחֲמָן הוּא יִשְׁלַח לָנוּ אֶת אֵלִיָּהוּ הַנָּבִיא זָכוּר לַטּוֹב, וִיבַשֶּׂר לָנוּ בְּשׂוֹרוֹת טוֹבוֹת יְשׁוּעוֹת וְנֶחָמוֹת. הָרַחֲמָן הוּא יְבָרֵךְ אֶת בַּעֲלִי / אִשְׁתִּי. הָרַחֲמָן הוּא יְבָרֵךְ אֶת אָבִי מוֹרִי [בַּעַל הַבַּיִת הַזֶּה]. וְאֶת אִמִּי מוֹרָתִי [בַּעֲלַת הַבַּיִת הַזֶּה], אוֹתָם וְאֶת בֵּיתָם וְאֶת זַרְעָם וְאֶת כָּל

אֲשֶׁר לָהֶם. אוֹתָנוּ וְאֶת כָּל אֲשֶׁר לָנוּ, כְּמוֹ שֶׁנִּתְבָּרְכוּ אֲבוֹתֵינוּ אַבְרָהָם יִצְחָק וְיַעֲקֹב בַּכֹּל מִכֹּל כֹּל, כֵּן יְבָרֵךְ אוֹתָנוּ כֻּלָּנוּ יַחַד בִּבְרָכָה שְׁלֵמָה, וְנֹאמַר, אָמֵן. בַּמָּרוֹם יְלַמְּדוּ עֲלֵיהֶם וְעָלֵינוּ זְכוּת שֶׁתְּהֵא לְמִשְׁמֶרֶת שָׁלוֹם. וְנִשָּׂא בְרָכָה מֵאֵת ה', וּצְדָקָה מֵאלֹהֵי יִשְׁעֵנוּ, וְנִמְצָא חֵן וְשֵׂכֶל טוֹב בְּעֵינֵי אֱלֹהִים וְאָדָם. בשבת: הָרַחֲמָן הוּא יַנְחִילֵנוּ יוֹם שֶׁכֻּלּוֹ שַׁבָּת וּמְנוּחָה לְחַיֵּי הָעוֹלָמִים. הָרַחֲמָן הוּא יַנְחִילֵנוּ יוֹם שֶׁכֻּלּוֹ טוֹב.[יוֹם שֶׁכֻּלּוֹ אָרוּךְ. יוֹם שֶׁצַּדִּיקִים יוֹשְׁבִים וְעַטְרוֹתֵיהֶם בְּרָאשֵׁיהֶם וְנֶהֱנִים מִזִּיו הַשְּׁכִינָה וִיהִי חֶלְקֵינוּ עִמָּהֶם.] הָרַחֲמָן הוּא יְזַכֵּנוּ לִימוֹת הַמָּשִׁיחַ וּלְחַיֵּי הָעוֹלָם הַבָּא. מִגְדּוֹל יְשׁוּעוֹת מַלְכּוֹ וְעֹשֶׂה חֶסֶד לִמְשִׁיחוֹ לְדָוִד וּלְזַרְעוֹ עַד עוֹלָם. עֹשֶׂה שָׁלוֹם בִּמְרוֹמָיו, הוּא יַעֲשֶׂה שָׁלוֹם עָלֵינוּ וְעַל כָּל יִשְׂרָאֵל וְאִמְרוּ, אָמֵן. יְראוּ אֶת ה' קְדֹשָׁיו, כִּי אֵין מַחְסוֹר לִירֵאָיו. כְּפִירִים רָשׁוּ וְרָעֵבוּ, וְדֹרְשֵׁי ה' לֹא יַחְסְרוּ כָל טוֹב. הוֹדוּ לַיי כִּי טוֹב כִּי לְעוֹלָם חַסְדּוֹ. פּוֹתֵחַ אֶת יָדֶךָ, וּמַשְׂבִּיעַ לְכָל חַי רָצוֹן. בָּרוּךְ הַגֶּבֶר אֲשֶׁר יִבְטַח בַּיי, וְהָיָה ה' מִבְטַחוֹ. נַעַר הָיִיתִי גַם זָקַנְתִּי, וְלֹא רָאִיתִי צַדִּיק נֶעֱזָב, וְזַרְעוֹ מְבַקֶּשׁ לָחֶם. יי עֹז לְעַמּוֹ יִתֵּן, ה', יְבָרֵךְ אֶת עַמּוֹ בַשָּׁלוֹם.

Birkat Hamazon

Explanation: Birkat Hamazon, the blessing after the meal, is also known colloquially as "benching," the English version of the Yiddish term bentshn, which means to bless.

This blessing (which is actually a series of blessings) is mandated for use following any meal in which bread has been eaten, since according to Jewish law, eating bread officially constitutes a meal. Birkat Hamazon can be said sitting at the same table or in view of the same table where the meal was eaten. At weddings or Shabbat meals, it is often said communally.[34]

We pour the third cup and recite the Grace over the Food.

(Directions: pour a cup of wine for all adults)

A Song of Ascents; When the Lord will bring back the captivity of Zion, we will be like dreamers. Then our mouth will be full of mirth and our tongue joyful melody; then they

[33] http://godtv.com. Accessed 3/30/2022.
[34] https://www.myjewishlearning.com/article/birkat-hamazon/. Accessed 3/30/2022.

will say among the nations; "The Lord has done greatly with these." The Lord has done great things with us; we are happy. Lord, return our captivity like streams in the desert. Those that sow with tears will reap with joyful song. He who surely goes and cries, he carries the measure of seed, he will surely come in joyful song and carry his sheaves. (Psalms 126)

Three that ate together are obligated to introduce the blessing and the leader of the introduction opens as follows:

My masters, let us bless.
  (All those present answer)
May the Name of the Lord be blessed from now and forever. (Psalms 113:2)
  (The leader says:)
With the permission of our gentlemen and our teachers and my masters, let us bless [our God] from whom we have eaten.
  (Those present answer:)
Blessed is [our God] from whom we have eaten and from whose goodness we live.
  (The leader repeats and says:)
Blessed is [our God] from whom we have eaten and from whose goodness we live.
  (They all say:)
Blessed are You, Lord our God, King of the Universe, who nourishes the entire world in His goodness, in grace, in kindness and in mercy; He gives bread to all flesh since His kindness is forever. And in His great goodness, we always have not lacked, and may we not lack nourishment forever and always, because of His great name. Since He is a Power that feeds and provides for all and does good to all and prepares nourishment for all of his creatures that he created. Blessed are You, Lord, who sustains all.

We thank you, Lord our God, that you have given as an inheritance to our ancestors a lovely, good and broad land, and that You took us out, Lord our God, from the land of Egypt and that You redeemed us from a house of slaves, and for Your covenant which You have sealed in our flesh, and for Your Torah that You have taught us, and for Your statutes which You have made known to us, and for life, grace and kindness that You have granted us and for the eating of nourishment that You feed and provide for us always, on all days, and at all times and in every hour.

And for everything, Lord our God, we thank You and bless You; may Your name be blessed by the mouth of all life, constantly forever and always, as it is written (Deuteronomy 8:10); "And you shall eat and you shall be satiated and you shall bless the Lord your God for the good land that He has given you." Blessed are You, Lord, for the land and for the nourishment.

Please have mercy, Lord our God, upon Israel, Your people; and upon Jerusalem, Your city; and upon Zion, the dwelling place of Your Glory; and upon the monarchy of the House of David, Your appointed one; and upon the great and holy house that Your name is called upon. Our God, our Father, tend us, sustain us, provide for us, relieve us and give us quick relief, Lord our God, from all of our troubles. And please do not make us needy, Lord our God, not for the gifts of flesh and blood, and not for their loans, but rather from Your full, open, holy and broad hand, so that we not be embarrassed and we not be ashamed forever and always.

(On Shabbat, we add the following paragraph)
May You be pleased to embolden us, Lord our God, in your commandments and in the command of the seventh day, of this great and holy Shabbat, since this day is great and holy before You, to cease work upon it and to rest upon it, with love, according to the

commandment of Your will. And with Your will, allow us, Lord our God, that we should not have trouble, and grief and sighing on the day of our rest. And may You show us, Lord our God, the consolation of Zion, Your city; and the building of Jerusalem, Your holy city; since You are the Master of salvations and the Master of consolations.

God and God of our ancestors, may there ascend and come and reach and be seen and be acceptable and be heard and be recalled and be remembered - our remembrance and our recollection; and the remembrance of our ancestors; and the remembrance of the messiah, the son of David, Your servant; and the remembrance of Jerusalem, Your holy city; and the remembrance of all Your people, the house of Israel - in front of You, for survival, for good, for grace, and for kindness, and for mercy, for life and for peace on this day of the Festival of Matzot. Remember us, Lord our God, on it for good and recall us on it for survival and save us on it for life, and by the word of salvation and mercy, pity and grace us and have mercy on us and save us, since our eyes are upon You, since You are a graceful and merciful Power. And may You build Jerusalem, the holy city, quickly and in our days. Blessed are You, Lord, who builds Jerusalem in His mercy. Amen.

Blessed are You, Lord our God, King of the Universe, the Power, our Father, our King, our Mighty One, our Creator, our Redeemer, our Shaper, our Holy One, the Holy One of Ya'akov, our Shepard, the Shepard of Israel, the good King, who does good to all, since on every single day He has done good, He does good, He will do good, to us; He has granted us, He grants us, He will grant us forever - in grace and in kindness, and in mercy, and in relief - rescue and success, blessing and salvation, consolation, provision and relief and mercy and life and peace and all good; and may we not lack any good ever.

May the Merciful One reign over us forever and always. May the Merciful One be blessed in the heavens and in the earth. May the Merciful One be praised for all generations, and exalted among us forever and ever, and glorified among us always and infinitely for all infinities. May the Merciful One sustain us honorably. May the Merciful One break our yolk from upon our necks and bring us upright to our land. May the Merciful One send us multiple blessing, to this home and upon this table upon which we have eaten. May the Merciful One send us Eliyahu the prophet - may he be remembered for good - and he shall announce to us tidings of good, of salvation and of consolation. May the Merciful One bless my husband/my wife. May the Merciful One bless [my father, my teacher,] the master of this home and [my mother, my teacher,] the mistress of this home, they and their home and their offspring and everything that is theirs. Us and all that is ours; as were blessed Avraham, Yitschak and Ya'akov, in everything, from everything, with everything, so too should He bless us, all of us together, with a complete blessing and we shall say, Amen. From above, may they advocate upon them and upon us merit, that should protect us in peace; and may we carry a blessing from the Lord and charity from the God of our salvation; and find grace and good understanding in the eyes of God and man. [On Shabbat, we say: May the Merciful One give us to inherit the day that will be completely Shabbat and rest in everlasting life.] May the Merciful One give us to inherit the day that will be all good. [The day that is all long, the day that the righteous will sit and their crowns will be on their heads and they will enjoy the radiance of the Divine presence and my our share be with them.] May the Merciful One give us merit for the times of the messiah and for life in the world to come. A tower of salvations is our King; may He do kindness with his messiah, with David and his offspring, forever (II Samuel 22:51). The One who makes peace above, may He make peace upon us and upon all of Israel; and say, Amen. Fear the Lord, His holy ones, since there is no lacking for those that fear Him. Young lions may go without and hunger, but those that seek the Lord will not lack any good thing (Psalms 34:10-11). Thank the Lord, since He is good, since His kindness is forever (Psalms 118:1). You open Your hand and satisfy the will of all living things (Psalms 146:16). Blessed is the man that trusts in the Lord and the Lord is his security (Jeremiah 17:7). I was a youth and I have also aged and I have not seen a righteous man forsaken and his offspring seeking bread (Psalms 37:25). The Lord will give courage to His people. The Lord will bless His people with peace (Psalms 29:11).

<u>הגדה של פסח ,ברך ,כוס שלישית א׳-ב׳</u>

בָּרוּךְ אַתָּה ה ,'אֱלֹהֵינוּ מֶלֶךְ הָעוֹלָם בּוֹרֵא פְּרִי הַגָּפֶן.

ושותים בהסיבה ואינו מברך ברכה אחרונה.

The third cup of Wine

Blessed are You, Lord our God, King of the universe, who creates the fruit of the vine.

(Directions: We drink while reclining and do not say a blessing afterward.)

הגדה של פסח ,ברך ,שפוך חמתך

מוזגים כוס של אליהו ופותחים את הדלת:

שְׁפֹךְ חֲמָתְךָ אֶל-הַגּוֹיִם אֲשֶׁר לֹא יְדָעוּךָ וְעַל-מַמְלָכוֹת אֲשֶׁר בְּשִׁמְךָ לֹא קָרָאוּ. כִּי אָכַל אֶת-יַעֲקֹב וְאֶת-נָוֵהוּ הֵשַׁמּוּ. שְׁפָךְ-עֲלֵיהֶם זַעְמֶךָ וַחֲרוֹן אַפְּךָ יַשִּׂיגֵם. תִּרְדֹּף בְּאַף וְתַשְׁמִידֵם מִתַּחַת שְׁמֵי ה'.

35 https://i.pinimg.com/originals/e7/f4/65/e7f465d929d04495aa78bdc300cb26ad.jpg. Accessed 3/30/2022.

[36]

Explanation: Elijah's cup, in Judaism, the fifth ceremonial cup of wine poured during the family seder dinner on Passover. It is left untouched in honor of Elijah, who, according to tradition, will arrive one day as an unknown guest to herald the advent of the messiah. During the seder dinner, biblical verses are read while the door is briefly opened to welcome Elijah, who, it is further said, will resolve all controversial questions connected with the Law. In this way the seder dinner not only commemorates the historical redemption from Egyptian bondage of the Jewish people (*see* Exodus) but also calls to mind their future redemption when Elijah and the messiah shall appear.[37]

We pour the cup of Eliyahu and open the door.

(Directions: open the main entrance to the house)

---

[36] http://the jerusalemgiftshop.com. Accessed 3/30/2022.

[37] https://www.britannica.com/topic/Elijahs-cup.. Accessed 3/30/2022.

Pour your wrath upon the nations that did not know You and upon the kingdoms that did not call upon Your Name! Since they have consumed Ya'akov and laid waste his habitation (Psalms 79:6-7). Pour out Your fury upon them and the fierceness of Your anger shall reach them (Psalms 69:25)! You shall pursue them with anger and eradicate them from under the skies of the Lord (Lamentations 3:66).

<u>הגדה של פסח ,הלל ,מסיימים את ההלל א'-י'</u>
הַלֵּל

לֹא לָנוּ ,ה ,'לֹא לָנוּ ,כִּי לְשִׁמְךָ תֵּן כָּבוֹד ,עַל חַסְדְּךָ עַל אֲמִתֶּךָ .לָמָּה יֹאמְרוּ הַגּוֹיִם אַיֵּה נָא אֱלֹהֵיהֶם וֵאלֹהֵינוּ בַשָּׁמַיִם ,כֹּל אֲשֶׁר חָפֵץ עָשָׂה .עֲצַבֵּיהֶם כֶּסֶף וְזָהָב מַעֲשֵׂה יְדֵי אָדָם .פֶּה לָהֶם וְלֹא יְדַבֵּרוּ ,עֵינַיִם לָהֶם וְלֹא יִרְאוּ .אָזְנַיִם לָהֶם וְלֹא יִשְׁמָעוּ ,אַף לָהֶם וְלֹא יְרִיחוּן .יְדֵיהֶם וְלֹא יְמִישׁוּן ,רַגְלֵיהֶם וְלֹא יְהַלֵּכוּ לֹא יֶהְגּוּ בִּגְרוֹנָם .כְּמוֹהֶם יִהְיוּ עֹשֵׂיהֶם ,כֹּל אֲשֶׁר בֹּטֵחַ בָּהֶם .יִשְׂרָאֵל בְּטַח בַּיי ,עֶזְרָם וּמָגִנָּם הוּא .בֵּית אַהֲרֹן בִּטְחוּ בַיי ,עֶזְרָם וּמָגִנָּם הוּא .יִרְאֵי ה 'בִּטְחוּ בַיי ,עֶזְרָם וּמָגִנָּם הוּא .יי זְכָרָנוּ יְבָרֵךְ .יְבָרֵךְ אֶת בֵּית יִשְׂרָאֵל ,יְבָרֵךְ אֶת בֵּית אַהֲרֹן ,יְבָרֵךְ יִרְאֵי ה ,'הַקְּטַנִּים עִם הַגְּדֹלִים .יֹסֵף ה 'עֲלֵיכֶם ,עֲלֵיכֶם וְעַל בְּנֵיכֶם בְּרוּכִים אַתֶּם לַיי ,עֹשֵׂה שָׁמַיִם וָאָרֶץ .הַשָּׁמַיִם שָׁמַיִם לַיי ,וְהָאָרֶץ נָתַן לִבְנֵי אָדָם .לֹא הַמֵּתִים יְהַלְלוּ יָהּ ,וְלֹא כָּל יֹרְדֵי דוּמָה .וַאֲנַחְנוּ נְבָרֵךְ יָהּ מֵעַתָּה וְעַד עוֹלָם .הַלְלוּיָהּ.

אָהַבְתִּי כִּי יִשְׁמַע ה 'אֶת קוֹלִי תַּחֲנוּנָי .כִּי הִטָּה אָזְנוֹ לִי וּבְיָמַי אֶקְרָא .אֲפָפוּנִי חֶבְלֵי מָוֶת וּמְצָרֵי שְׁאוֹל מְצָאוּנִי ,צָרָה וְיָגוֹן אֶמְצָא .וּבְשֵׁם ה 'אֶקְרָא :אָנָּה ה 'מַלְּטָה נַפְשִׁי .חַנּוּן ה 'וְצַדִּיק ,וֵאלֹהֵינוּ מְרַחֵם .שֹׁמֵר פְּתָאִים ה ,'דַּלּוֹתִי וְלִי יְהוֹשִׁיעַ .שׁוּבִי נַפְשִׁי לִמְנוּחָיְכִי ,כִּי ה 'גָּמַל עָלָיְכִי .כִּי חִלַּצְתָּ נַפְשִׁי מִמָּוֶת ,אֶת עֵינִי מִן דִּמְעָה ,אֶת רַגְלִי מִדֶּחִי .אֶתְהַלֵּךְ לִפְנֵי ה 'בְּאַרְצוֹת הַחַיִּים .הֶאֱמַנְתִּי כִּי אֲדַבֵּר ,אֲנִי עָנִיתִי מְאֹד .אֲנִי אָמַרְתִּי בְחָפְזִי כָּל הָאָדָם כֹּזֵב.

מָה אָשִׁיב לַיי כֹּל תַּגְמוּלוֹהִי עָלָי .כּוֹס יְשׁוּעוֹת אֶשָּׂא וּבְשֵׁם ה 'אֶקְרָא .נְדָרַי לַיי אֲשַׁלֵּם נֶגְדָה נָּא לְכָל עַמּוֹ יָקָר בְּעֵינֵי ה 'הַמָּוְתָה לַחֲסִידָיו .אָנָּה ה 'כִּי אֲנִי עַבְדֶּךָ ,אֲנִי עַבְדְּךָ בֶּן אֲמָתֶךָ ,פִּתַּחְתָּ לְמוֹסֵרָי .לְךָ אֶזְבַּח זֶבַח תּוֹדָה וּבְשֵׁם ה 'אֶקְרָא .נְדָרַי לַיי אֲשַׁלֵּם נֶגְדָה נָּא לְכָל עַמּוֹ .בְּחַצְרוֹת בֵּית ה ,'בְּתוֹכֵכִי יְרוּשָׁלָיִם .הַלְלוּיָהּ הַלְלוּ אֶת ה 'כָּל גּוֹיִם ,שַׁבְּחוּהוּ כָּל הָאֻמִּים .כִּי גָבַר עָלֵינוּ חַסְדּוֹ ,וֶאֱמֶת ה 'לְעוֹלָם .הַלְלוּיָהּ .הוֹדוּ לַיי כִּי טוֹב כִּי לְעוֹלָם חַסְדּוֹ .יֹאמַר נָא יִשְׂרָאֵל כִּי לְעוֹלָם חַסְדּוֹ .יֹאמְרוּ נָא בֵית אַהֲרֹן כִּי לְעוֹלָם חַסְדּוֹ .יֹאמְרוּ נָא יִרְאֵי ה 'כִּי לְעוֹלָם חַסְדּוֹ.

מִן הַמֵּצַר קָרָאתִי יָּהּ ,עָנָנִי בַמֶּרְחָב יָהּ .ה 'לִי ,לֹא אִירָא - מַה יַּעֲשֶׂה לִי אָדָם ,ה 'לִי בְּעֹזְרָי וַאֲנִי אֶרְאֶה בְשֹׂנְאָי .טוֹב לַחֲסוֹת בַּיי מִבְּטֹחַ בָּאָדָם .טוֹב לַחֲסוֹת בַּיי מִבְּטֹחַ בִּנְדִיבִים .כָּל גּוֹיִם סְבָבוּנִי ,בְּשֵׁם ה 'כִּי אֲמִילַם .סַבּוּנִי גַם סְבָבוּנִי ,בְּשֵׁם ה 'כִּי אֲמִילַם .סַבּוּנִי כִדְבֹרִים ,דֹּעֲכוּ כְּאֵשׁ קוֹצִים ,בְּשֵׁם ה 'כִּי אֲמִילַם .דָּחֹה דְחִיתַנִי לִנְפֹּל ,וַיי עֲזָרָנִי .עָזִּי וְזִמְרָת יָהּ וַיְהִי לִי לִישׁוּעָה .קוֹל רִנָּה וִישׁוּעָה בְּאָהֳלֵי צַדִּיקִים :יְמִין ה 'עֹשָׂה חָיִל ,יְמִין ה 'רוֹמֵמָה ,יְמִין ה 'עֹשָׂה חָיִל .לֹא אָמוּת כִּי אֶחְיֶה ,וַאֲסַפֵּר מַעֲשֵׂי יָהּ .יַסֹּר יִסְּרַנִּי יָּהּ ,וְלַמָּוֶת לֹא נְתָנָנִי .פִּתְחוּ לִי שַׁעֲרֵי צֶדֶק ,אָבֹא בָם ,אוֹדֶה יָהּ .זֶה הַשַּׁעַר לַיי ,צַדִּיקִים יָבֹאוּ בוֹ אוֹדְךָ כִּי עֲנִיתָנִי וַתְּהִי לִי לִישׁוּעָה .אוֹדְךָ כִּי עֲנִיתָנִי וַתְּהִי לִי לִישׁוּעָה .אֶבֶן מָאֲסוּ הַבּוֹנִים הָיְתָה לְרֹאשׁ פִּנָּה אֶבֶן מָאֲסוּ הַבּוֹנִים הָיְתָה לְרֹאשׁ פִּנָּה .מֵאֵת ה 'הָיְתָה זֹּאת הִיא נִפְלָאת בְּעֵינֵינוּ .מֵאֵת ה 'הָיְתָה זֹּאת הִיא נִפְלָאת בְּעֵינֵינוּ

אָנָּא ה', הוֹשִׁיעָה נָּא .אָנָּא ה', הוֹשִׁיעָה נָּא .אָנָּא ה', הַצְלִיחָה נָא .אָנָּא ה', הַצְלִיחָה נָא .אָנָּא ה', הַצְלִיחָה נָא .
בָּרוּךְ הַבָּא בְּשֵׁם ה', בֵּרַכְנוּכֶם מִבֵּית ה' .בָּרוּךְ הַבָּא בְּשֵׁם ה', בֵּרַכְנוּכֶם מִבֵּית ה' .אֵל ה' וַיָּאֶר לָנוּ .אִסְרוּ
חַג בַּעֲבֹתִים עַד קַרְנוֹת הַמִּזְבֵּחַ .אֵל ה' וַיָּאֶר לָנוּ .אִסְרוּ חַג בַּעֲבֹתִים עַד קַרְנוֹת הַמִּזְבֵּחַ .אֵלִי אַתָּה וְאוֹדֶךָּ,
אֱלֹהַי - אֲרוֹמְמֶךָּ .אֵלִי אַתָּה וְאוֹדֶךָּ, אֱלֹהַי - אֲרוֹמְמֶךָּ .הוֹדוּ לַיי כִּי טוֹב, כִּי לְעוֹלָם חַסְדּוֹ .הוֹדוּ לַיי כִּי טוֹב
כִּי לְעוֹלָם חַסְדּוֹ .
יְהַלְלוּךָ ה' אֱלֹהֵינוּ כָּל מַעֲשֶׂיךָ, וַחֲסִידֶיךָ צַדִּיקִים עוֹשֵׂי רְצוֹנֶךָ, וְכָל עַמְּךָ בֵּית יִשְׂרָאֵל בְּרִנָּה יוֹדוּ וִיבָרְכוּ
וִישַׁבְּחוּ וִיפָאֲרוּ, וִירוֹמְמוּ וְיַעֲרִיצוּ, וְיַקְדִּישׁוּ וְיַמְלִיכוּ אֶת שִׁמְךָ, מַלְכֵּנוּ .כִּי לְךָ טוֹב לְהוֹדוֹת וּלְשִׁמְךָ נָאֶה
לְזַמֵּר, כִּי מֵעוֹלָם וְעַד עוֹלָם אַתָּה אֵל .

Second Half of the Hallel

Not to us, not to us, but rather to Your name, give glory for your kindness and for your truth. Why should the nations say, "Say, where is their God?" But our God is in the heavens, all that He wanted, He has done. Their idols are silver and gold, the work of men's hands. They have a mouth but do not speak; they have eyes but do not see. They have ears but do not hear; they have a nose but do not smell. Hands, but they do not feel; feet, but do not walk; they do not make a peep from their throat. Like them will be their makers, all those that trust in them. Israel, trust in the Lord; their help and shield is He. House of Aharon, trust in the Lord; their help and shield is He. Those that fear the Lord, trust in the Lord; their help and shield is He. The Lord who remembers us, will bless; He will bless the House of Israel; He will bless the House of Aharon. He will bless those that fear the Lord, the small ones with the great ones. May the Lord bring increase to you, to you and to your children. Blessed are you to the Lord, the maker of the heavens and the earth. The heavens, are the Lord's heavens, but the earth He has given to the children of man. It is not the dead that will praise the Lord, and

---

[38] http://youtube.com. Acccessed 3/30/2022.

not those that go down to silence. But we will bless the Lord from now and forever. Halleluyah! (Psalms 115)

I have loved the Lord - since He hears my voice, my supplications. Since He inclined His ear to me - and in my days, I will call out. The pangs of death have encircled me and the straits of the Pit have found me and I found grief. And in the name of the Lord I called, "Please Lord, Spare my soul." Gracious is the Lord and righteous, and our God acts mercifully. The Lord watches over the silly; I was poor and He has saved me. Return, my soul to your tranquility, since the Lord has favored you. Since You have rescued my soul from death, my eyes from tears, my feet from stumbling. I will walk before the Lord in the lands of the living. I have trusted, when I speak - I am very afflicted. I said in my haste, all men are hypocritical. (Psalms 116:1-11)

What can I give back to the Lord for all that He has favored me? A cup of salvations I will raise up and I will call out in the name of the Lord. My vows to the Lord I will pay, now in front of His entire people. Precious in the eyes of the Lord is the death of His pious ones. Please Lord, since I am Your servant, the son of Your maidservant; You have opened my chains. To You will I offer a thanksgiving offering and I will call out in the name of the Lord. My vows to the Lord I will pay, now in front of His entire people. In the courtyards of the house of the Lord, in your midst, Jerusalem. Halleluyah! (Psalms 116:12-19)

Praise the name of the Lord, all nations; extol Him all peoples. Since His kindness has overwhelmed us and the truth of the Lord is forever. Halleluyah! Thank the Lord, since He is good, since His kindness is forever. Let Israel now said, "Thank the Lord, since He is good, since His kindness is forever." Let the House of Aharon now said, "Thank the Lord, since He is good, since His kindness is forever." Let those that fear the Lord now said, "Thank the Lord, since He is good, since His kindness is forever." (Psalms 117-118:4)

From the strait I have called, Lord; He answered me from the wide space, the Lord. The Lord is for me, I will not fear, what will man do to me? The Lord is for me with my helpers, and I shall glare at those that hate me. It is better to take refuge with the Lord than to trust in man. It is better to take refuge with the Lord than to trust in nobles. All the nations surrounded me - in the name of the Lord, as I will chop them off. They surrounded me, they also encircled me - in the name of the Lord, as I will chop them off. They surrounded me like bees, they were extinguished like a fire of thorns - in the name of the Lord, as I will chop them off. You have surely pushed me to fall, but the Lord helped me. My boldness and song is the Lord, and He has become my salvation. The sound of happy song and salvation is in the tents of the righteous, the right hand of the Lord acts powerfully. I will not die but rather I will live and tell over the acts of the Lord. The Lord has surely chastised me, but He has not given me over to death. Open up for me the gates of righteousness; I will enter them, thank the Lord. This is the gate of the Lord, the righteous will enter it. (Psalms 118:5-20)
I will thank You, since You answered me and You have become my salvation. The stone that was left by the builders has become the main cornerstone. From the Lord was this, it is wondrous in our eyes. This is the day of the Lord, let us exult and rejoice upon it. (Psalms 118:21-24)

Please, Lord, save us now; please, Lord, give us success now! (Psalms 118:25)

Blessed be the one who comes in the name of the Lord, we have blessed you from the house of the Lord. God is the Lord, and He has illuminated us; tie up the festival offering with ropes until it reaches the corners of the altar. You are my Power and I will

Thank You; my God and I will exalt You. Thank the Lord, since He is good, since His kindness is forever. (Psalms 118:26-29)

All of your works shall praise You, Lord our God, and your pious ones, the righteous ones who do Your will; and all of Your people, the House of Israel will thank and bless in joyful song: and extol and glorify, and exalt and acclaim, and sanctify and coronate Your name, our King. Since, You it is good to thank, and to Your name it is pleasant to sing, since from always and forever are you the Power.

הגדה של פסח ,הלל ,מזמורי הודיה א'-ו'

הוֹדוּ לַיי כִּי טוֹב כִּי לְעוֹלָם חַסְדּוֹ .הוֹדוּ לֵאלֹהֵי הָאֱלֹהִים כִּי לְעוֹלָם חַסְדּוֹ .הוֹדוּ לַאֲדֹנֵי הָאֲדֹנִים כִּי לְעוֹלָם חַסְדּוֹ .לְעֹשֵׂה נִפְלָאוֹת גְּדֹלוֹת לְבַדּוֹ כִּי לְעוֹלָם חַסְדּוֹ .לְעֹשֵׂה הַשָּׁמַיִם בִּתְבוּנָה כִּי לְעוֹלָם חַסְדּוֹ .לְרוֹקַע הָאָרֶץ עַל הַמָּיִם כִּי לְעוֹלָם חַסְדּוֹ .לְעֹשֵׂה אוֹרִים גְּדֹלִים כִּי לְעוֹלָם חַסְדּוֹ .אֶת הַשֶּׁמֶשׁ לְמֶמְשֶׁלֶת בַּיּוֹם כִּי לְעוֹלָם חַסְדּוֹ .אֶת הַיָּרֵחַ וְכוֹכָבִים לְמֶמְשְׁלוֹת בַּלַּיְלָה כִּי לְעוֹלָם חַסְדּוֹ .לְמַכֵּה מִצְרַיִם בִּבְכוֹרֵיהֶם כִּי לְעוֹלָם חַסְדּוֹ .וַיּוֹצֵא יִשְׂרָאֵל מִתּוֹכָם כִּי לְעוֹלָם חַסְדּוֹ .בְּיָד חֲזָקָה וּבִזְרוֹעַ נְטוּיָה כִּי לְעוֹלָם חַסְדּוֹ.לְגֹזֵר יַם סוּף לִגְזָרִים כִּי לְעוֹלָם חַסְדּוֹ .וְהֶעֱבִיר יִשְׂרָאֵל בְּתוֹכוֹ כִּי לְעוֹלָם חַסְדּוֹ .וְנִעֵר פַּרְעֹה וְחֵילוֹ בְיַם סוּף כִּי לְעוֹלָם חַסְדּוֹ .לְמוֹלִיךְ עַמּוֹ בַּמִּדְבָּר כִּי לְעוֹלָם חַסְדּוֹ .לְמַכֵּה מְלָכִים גְּדֹלִים כִּי לְעוֹלָם חַסְדּוֹ .וַיַּהֲרֹג מְלָכִים אַדִּירִים כִּי לְעוֹלָם חַסְדּוֹ .לְסִיחוֹן מֶלֶךְ הָאֱמֹרִי כִּי לְעוֹלָם חַסְדּוֹ .וּלְעוֹג מֶלֶךְ הַבָּשָׁן כִּי לְעוֹלָם חַסְדּוֹ .וְנָתַן אַרְצָם לְנַחֲלָה כִּי לְעוֹלָם חַסְדּוֹ .נַחֲלָה לְיִשְׂרָאֵל עַבְדּוֹ כִּי לְעוֹלָם חַסְדּוֹ .שֶׁבְּשִׁפְלֵנוּ זָכַר לָנוּ כִּי לְעוֹלָם חַסְדּוֹ .וַיִּפְרְקֵנוּ מִצָּרֵינוּ כִּי לְעוֹלָם חַסְדּוֹ .נֹתֵן לֶחֶם לְכָל בָּשָׂר כִּי לְעוֹלָם חַסְדּוֹ .הוֹדוּ לְאֵל הַשָּׁמַיִם כִּי לְעוֹלָם חַסְדּוֹ.

נִשְׁמַת כָּל חַי תְּבָרֵךְ אֶת שִׁמְךָ, ה' אֱלֹהֵינוּ ,וְרוּחַ כָּל בָּשָׂר תְּפָאֵר וּתְרוֹמֵם זִכְרְךָ, מַלְכֵּנוּ ,תָמִיד .מִן הָעוֹלָם וְעַד הָעוֹלָם אַתָּה אֵל ,וּמִבַּלְעָדֶיךָ אֵין לָנוּ מֶלֶךְ גּוֹאֵל וּמוֹשִׁיעַ ,פּוֹדֶה וּמַצִּיל וּמְפַרְנֵס וּמְרַחֵם בְּכָל עֵת צָרָה וְצוּקָה .אֵין לָנוּ מֶלֶךְ אֶלָּא אַתָּה .אֱלֹהֵי הָרִאשׁוֹנִים וְהָאַחֲרוֹנִים ,אֱלוֹהַּ כָּל בְּרִיּוֹת ,אֲדוֹן כָּל תּוֹלָדוֹת ,הַמְהֻלָּל בְּרֹב הַתִּשְׁבָּחוֹת ,הַמְנַהֵג עוֹלָמוֹ בְּחֶסֶד וּבְרִיּוֹתָיו בְּרַחֲמִים .וַיי לֹא יָנוּם וְלֹא יִישָׁן - הַמְעוֹרֵר יְשֵׁנִים וְהַמֵּקִיץ נִרְדָּמִים ,וְהַמֵּשִׂיחַ אִלְּמִים וְהַמַּתִּיר אֲסוּרִים וְהַסּוֹמֵךְ נוֹפְלִים וְהַזּוֹקֵף כְּפוּפִים לְךָ לְבַדְּךָ אֲנַחְנוּ מוֹדִים.

אִלּוּ פִינוּ מָלֵא שִׁירָה כַּיָּם ,וּלְשׁוֹנֵנוּ רִנָּה כַּהֲמוֹן גַּלָּיו ,וְשִׂפְתוֹתֵינוּ שֶׁבַח כְּמֶרְחֲבֵי רָקִיעַ ,וְעֵינֵינוּ מְאִירוֹת כַּשֶּׁמֶשׁ וְכַיָּרֵחַ ,וְיָדֵינוּ פְרוּשׂוֹת כְּנִשְׁרֵי שָׁמָיִם ,וְרַגְלֵינוּ קַלּוֹת כָּאַיָּלוֹת - אֵין אֲנַחְנוּ מַסְפִּיקִים לְהוֹדוֹת לְךָ ,ה' אֱלֹהֵינוּ וֵאלֹהֵי אֲבוֹתֵינוּ ,וּלְבָרֵךְ אֶת שִׁמְךָ עַל אַחַת מֵאֶלֶף ,אַלְפֵי אֲלָפִים וְרִבֵּי רְבָבוֹת פְּעָמִים הַטּוֹבוֹת שֶׁעָשִׂיתָ עִם אֲבוֹתֵינוּ וְעִמָּנוּ .מִמִּצְרַיִם גְּאַלְתָּנוּ ,ה' אֱלֹהֵינוּ ,וּמִבֵּית עֲבָדִים פְּדִיתָנוּ ,בְּרָעָב זַנְתָּנוּ וּבְשָׂבָע כִּלְכַּלְתָּנוּ ,מֵחֶרֶב הִצַּלְתָּנוּ וּמִדֶּבֶר מִלַּטְתָּנוּ ,וּמֵחֳלָיִם רָעִים וְנֶאֱמָנִים דִּלִּיתָנוּ.

עַד הֵנָּה עֲזָרוּנוּ רַחֲמֶיךָ וְלֹא עֲזָבוּנוּ חֲסָדֶיךָ ,וְאַל תִּטְּשֵׁנוּ ,ה' אֱלֹהֵינוּ ,לָנֶצַח .עַל כֵּן אֵבָרִים שֶׁפִּלַּגְתָּ בָּנוּ וְרוּחַ וּנְשָׁמָה שֶׁנָּפַחְתָּ בְּאַפֵּינוּ וְלָשׁוֹן אֲשֶׁר שַׂמְתָּ בְּפִינוּ - הֵן הֵם יוֹדוּ וִיבָרְכוּ וִישַׁבְּחוּ וִיפָאֲרוּ וִירוֹמְמוּ וְיַעֲרִיצוּ

וְיַקְדִּישׁוּ וְיַמְלִיכוּ אֶת שִׁמְךָ מַלְכֵּנוּ. כִּי כָל פֶּה לְךָ יוֹדֶה, וְכָל לָשׁוֹן לְךָ תִּשָּׁבַע, וְכָל בֶּרֶךְ לְךָ תִכְרַע, וְכָל
קוֹמָה לְפָנֶיךָ תִשְׁתַּחֲוֶה, וְכָל לְבָבוֹת יִירָאוּךָ, וְכָל קֶרֶב וּכְלָיוֹת יְזַמְּרוּ לִשְׁמֶךָ. כַּדָּבָר שֶׁכָּתוּב, כָּל עַצְמוֹתַי
תֹּאמַרְנָה, ה' מִי כָמוֹךָ מַצִּיל עָנִי מֵחָזָק מִמֶּנּוּ וְעָנִי וְאֶבְיוֹן מִגֹּזְלוֹ. מִי יִדְמֶה לָּךְ וּמִי יִשְׁוֶה לָּךְ וּמִי יַעֲרָךְ לָךְ
הָאֵל הַגָּדוֹל, הַגִּבּוֹר וְהַנּוֹרָא, אֵל עֶלְיוֹן, קֹנֵה שָׁמַיִם וָאָרֶץ. נְהַלֶּלְךָ וּנְשַׁבֵּחֲךָ וּנְפָאֶרְךָ וּנְבָרֵךְ אֶת שֵׁם קָדְשֶׁךָ
כָּאָמוּר: לְדָוִד, בָּרְכִי נַפְשִׁי אֶת ה' וְכָל קְרָבַי אֶת שֵׁם קָדְשׁוֹ. הָאֵל בְּתַעֲצֻמוֹת עֻזֶּךָ, הַגָּדוֹל בִּכְבוֹד שְׁמֶךָ
הַגִּבּוֹר לָנֶצַח וְהַנּוֹרָא בְּנוֹרְאוֹתֶיךָ, הַמֶּלֶךְ הַיּוֹשֵׁב עַל כִּסֵּא רָם וְנִשָּׂא. שׁוֹכֵן עַד מָרוֹם וְקָדוֹשׁ שְׁמוֹ. וְכָתוּב:
רַנְּנוּ צַדִּיקִים בַּיְיָ, לַיְשָׁרִים נָאוָה תְהִלָּה. בְּפִי יְשָׁרִים תִּתְהַלָּל, וּבְדִבְרֵי צַדִּיקִים תִּתְבָּרַךְ, וּבִלְשׁוֹן חֲסִידִים
תִּתְרוֹמָם, וּבְקֶרֶב קְדוֹשִׁים תִּתְקַדָּשׁ.
וּבְמַקְהֲלוֹת רִבְבוֹת עַמְּךָ בֵּית יִשְׂרָאֵל בְּרִנָּה יִתְפָּאֵר שִׁמְךָ, מַלְכֵּנוּ, בְּכָל דּוֹר וָדוֹר, שֶׁכֵּן חוֹבַת כָּל הַיְצוּרִים
לְפָנֶיךָ, ה' אֱלֹהֵינוּ וֵאלֹהֵי אֲבוֹתֵינוּ, לְהוֹדוֹת לְהַלֵּל לְשַׁבֵּחַ, לְפָאֵר לְרוֹמֵם לְהַדֵּר לְבָרֵךְ, לְעַלֵּה וּלְקַלֵּס עַל
כָּל דִּבְרֵי שִׁירוֹת וְתִשְׁבְּחוֹת דָּוִד בֶּן יִשַׁי עַבְדְּךָ מְשִׁיחֶךָ.
יִשְׁתַּבַּח שִׁמְךָ לָעַד מַלְכֵּנוּ, הָאֵל הַמֶּלֶךְ הַגָּדוֹל וְהַקָּדוֹשׁ בַּשָּׁמַיִם וּבָאָרֶץ, כִּי לְךָ נָאֶה, ה', אֱלֹהֵינוּ וֵאלֹהֵי
אֲבוֹתֵינוּ, שִׁיר וּשְׁבָחָה, הַלֵּל וְזִמְרָה, עֹז וּמֶמְשָׁלָה, נֶצַח, גְּדֻלָּה וּגְבוּרָה, תְּהִלָּה וְתִפְאֶרֶת, קְדֻשָּׁה וּמַלְכוּת
בְּרָכוֹת וְהוֹדָאוֹת מֵעַתָּה וְעַד עוֹלָם. בָּרוּךְ אַתָּה ה', אֵל מֶלֶךְ גָּדוֹל בַּתִּשְׁבָּחוֹת, אֵל הַהוֹדָאוֹת, אֲדוֹן
הַנִּפְלָאוֹת, הַבּוֹחֵר בְּשִׁירֵי זִמְרָה, מֶלֶךְ אֵל חֵי הָעוֹלָמִים.

Thank the Lord, since He is good, since His kindness is forever. Thank the Power of powers since His kindness is forever. To the Master of masters, since His kindness is forever. To the One who alone does wondrously great deeds, since His kindness is forever. To the one who made the Heavens with discernment, since His kindness is forever. To the One who spread the earth over the waters, since His kindness is forever. To the One who made great lights, since His kindness is forever. The sun to rule in the day, since His kindness is forever. The moon and the stars to rule in the night, since His kindness is forever. To the One that smote Egypt through their firstborn, since His kindness is forever. And He took Israel out from among them, since His kindness is forever. With a strong hand and an outstretched forearm, since His kindness is forever. To the One who cut up the Reed Sea into strips, since His kindness is forever. And He made Israel to pass through it, since His kindness is forever. And He jolted Pharaoh and his troop in the Reed Sea, since His kindness is forever. To the One who led his people in the wilderness, since His kindness is forever. To the One who smote great kings, since His kindness is forever. And he killed mighty kings, since His kindness is forever. Sichon, king of the Amorite, since His kindness is forever. And Og, king of the Bashan, since His kindness is forever. And he gave their land as an inheritance, since

---

39 http://greenbankglasgow.org.uk. Accessed 3/30/2022.

His kindness is forever. An inheritance for Israel, His servant, since His kindness is forever. That in our lowliness, He remembered us, since His kindness is forever. And he delivered us from our adversaries, since His kindness is forever. He gives bread to all flesh, since His kindness is forever. Thank the Power of the heavens, since His kindness is forever. (Psalms 136)

The soul of every living being shall bless Your Name, Lord our God; the spirit of all flesh shall glorify and exalt Your remembrance always, our King. From the world and until the world, You are the Power, and other than You we have no king, redeemer, or savior, restorer, rescuer, provider, and merciful one in every time of distress and anguish; we have no king, besides You! God of the first ones and the last ones, God of all creatures, Master of all Generations, Who is praised through a multitude of praises, Who guides His world with kindness and His creatures with mercy. The Lord neither slumbers nor sleeps. He who rouses the sleepers and awakens the dozers; He who makes the mute speak, and frees the captives, and supports the falling, and straightens the bent. We thank You alone.

Were our mouth as full of song as the sea, and our tongue as full of joyous song as its multitude of waves, and our lips as full of praise as the breadth of the heavens, and our eyes as sparkling as the sun and the moon, and our hands as outspread as the eagles of the sky and our feet as swift as deers - we still could not thank You sufficiently, Lord our God and God of our ancestors, and to bless Your Name for one thousandth of the thousand of thousands of thousands, and myriad myriads, of goodnesses that You performed for our ancestors and for us. From Egypt, Lord our God, did you redeem us and from the house of slaves you restored us. In famine You nourished us, and in plenty you sustained us. From the sword you saved us, and from plague you spared us; and from severe and enduring diseases you delivered us.

Until now Your mercy has helped us, and Your kindness has not forsaken us; and do not abandon us, Lord our God, forever. Therefore, the limbs that You set within us and the spirit and soul that You breathed into our nostrils, and the tongue that You placed in our mouth - verily, they shall thank and bless and praise and glorify, and exalt and revere, and sanctify and coronate Your name, our King. For every mouth shall offer thanks to You; and every tongue shall swear allegiance to You; and every knee shall bend to You; and every upright one shall prostrate himself before You; all hearts shall fear You; and all innermost feelings and thoughts shall sing praises to Your name, as the matter is written (Psalms 35:10), "All my bones shall say, 'Lord, who is like You? You save the poor man from one who is stronger than he, the poor and destitute from the one who would rob him.'" Who is similar to You and who is equal to You and who can be compared to You, O great, strong and awesome Power, O highest Power, Creator of the heavens and the earth. We shall praise and extol and glorify and bless Your holy name, as it is stated (Psalms 103:1), " [A Psalm] of David. Bless the Lord, O my soul; and all that is within me, His holy name." The Power, in Your powerful boldness; the Great, in the glory of Your name; the Strong One forever; the King who sits on His high and elevated throne. He who dwells always; lofty and holy is His name. And as it is written (Psalms 33:10), "Sing joyfully to the Lord, righteous ones, praise is beautiful from the upright." By the mouth of the upright You shall be praised; By the lips of the righteous shall You be blessed; By the tongue of the devout shall You be exalted; And among the holy shall You be sanctified.

And in the assemblies of the myriads of Your people, the House of Israel, in joyous song will Your name be glorified, our King, in each and every generation; as it is the duty of all creatures, before You, Lord our God, and God of our ancestors, to thank, to praise, to extol, to glorify, to exalt, to lavish, to bless, to raise high and to acclaim - beyond the words of the songs and praises of David, the son of Yishai, Your servant, Your anointed one.

May Your name be praised forever, our King, the Power, the Great and holy King - in the heavens and in the earth. Since for You it is pleasant - O Lord our God and God of our ancestors - song and lauding, praise and hymn, boldness and dominion, triumph, greatness and strength, psalm and splendor, holiness and kingship, blessings and thanksgivings, from now and forever. Blessed are You Lord, Power, King exalted through laudings, Power of thanksgivings, Master of Wonders, who chooses the songs of hymn - King, Power of the life of the worlds.

<u>הגדה של פסח ,הלל ,כוס רביעית א'-ד'</u>

בָּרוּךְ אַתָּה ה' ,אֱלֹהֵינוּ מֶלֶךְ הָעוֹלָם בּוֹרֵא פְּרִי הַגָּפֶן.

וְשׁוֹתֶה בַּהֲסִיבַת שְׂמֹאל.

בָּרוּךְ אַתָּה ה' אֱלֹהֵינוּ מֶלֶךְ הָעוֹלָם ,עַל הַגֶּפֶן וְעַל פְּרִי הַגֶּפֶן ,עַל תְּנוּבַת הַשָּׂדֶה וְעַל אֶרֶץ חֶמְדָּה טוֹבָה וּרְחָבָה שֶׁרָצִיתָ וְהִנְחַלְתָּ לַאֲבוֹתֵינוּ לֶאֱכוֹל מִפִּרְיָהּ וְלִשְׂבֹּעַ מִטּוּבָהּ .רַחֶם נָא ה' אֱלֹהֵינוּ עַל יִשְׂרָאֵל עַמֶּךָ וְעַל יְרוּשָׁלַיִם עִירֶךָ וְעַל צִיּוֹן מִשְׁכַּן כְּבוֹדֶךָ וְעַל מִזְבְּחֶךָ וְעַל הֵיכָלֶךָ וּבְנֵה יְרוּשָׁלַיִם עִיר הַקֹּדֶשׁ בִּמְהֵרָה בְיָמֵינוּ וְהַעֲלֵנוּ לְתוֹכָהּ וְשַׂמְּחֵנוּ בְּבִנְיָנָהּ וְנֹאכַל מִפִּרְיָהּ וְנִשְׂבַּע מִטּוּבָהּ וּנְבָרֶכְךָ עָלֶיהָ בִּקְדֻשָּׁה וּבְטָהֳרָה [בשבת :וּרְצֵה וְהַחֲלִיצֵנוּ בְּיוֹם הַשַּׁבָּת הַזֶּה] ,וְשַׂמְּחֵנוּ בְּיוֹם חַג הַמַּצּוֹת הַזֶּה ,כִּי אַתָּה ה' טוֹב וּמֵטִיב לַכֹּל וְנוֹדֶה לְךָ עַל הָאָרֶץ וְעַל פְּרִי הַגָּפֶן.

בָּרוּךְ אַתָּה ה' ,עַל הַגֶּפֶן וְעַל פְּרִי הַגָּפֶן.

Fourth Cup of Wine

(Directions: Pour a cup of wine)

Blessed are You, Lord our God, King of the universe, who creates the fruit of the vine. We drink while reclining to the left.

Blessed are You, Lord our God, King of the universe, for the vine and for the fruit of the vine; and for the bounty of the field; and for a desirable, good and broad land, which You wanted to give to our fathers, to eat from its fruit and to be satiated from its goodness. Please have mercy, Lord our God upon Israel Your people; and upon Jerusalem, Your city: and upon Zion, the dwelling place of Your glory; and upon Your altar; and upon Your sanctuary; and build Jerusalem Your holy city quickly in our days, and bring us up into it and gladden us in its building; and we shall eat from its fruit, and be satiated from its goodness, and bless You in holiness and purity. [On Shabbat: And may you be pleased to embolden us on this Shabbat day] and gladden us on this day of the Festival of Matzot. Since You, Lord, are good and do good to all, we thank You for the land and for the fruit of the vine.

Blessed are You, Lord, for the land and for the fruit of the vine

---

[40] http://curtlandry.com/. Accessed 3/30/2022.

נִרְצָה

חֲסַל סִדּוּר פֶּסַח כְּהִלְכָתוֹ ,כְּכָל מִשְׁפָּטוֹ וְחֻקָּתוֹ .כַּאֲשֶׁר זָכִינוּ לְסַדֵּר אוֹתוֹ כֵּן נִזְכֶּה לַעֲשׂוֹתוֹ .זָךְ שׁוֹכֵן מְעוֹנָה ,קוֹמֵם קְהַל עֲדַת מִי מָנָה .בְּקָרוֹב נַהֵל נִטְעֵי כַנָּה פְּדוּיִם לְצִיּוֹן בְּרִנָּה.

Completed is the Seder of Pesach according to its law, according to all its judgment and statute. Just as we have merited to arrange it, so too, may we merit to do [its sacrifice]. Pure One who dwells in the habitation, raise up the congregation of the community, which whom can count. Bring close, lead the plantings of the sapling, redeemed, to Zion in joy.

הגדה של פסח ,נרצה ,לשנה הבאה א'
.לְשָׁנָה הַבָּאָה בִּירוּשָׁלָיִם הַבְּנוּיָה

L'Shana HaBaa

L'Shana Haba'ah B'Yerushalayim (Hebrew: לשנה הבאה בירושלים), lit. "Next year in Jerusalem", is a phrase that is often sung at the end of the Passover Seder and at the end of the Ne'ila service on Yom Kippur. Its use during Passover was first recorded by Isaac Tyrnau in his 15th century CE book cataloging the Minhaggim of various Ashkenazi communities.

Next year, let us be in the built Jerusalem!

<u>הגדה של פסח ,נרצה ,ויהי בחצי הלילה א'-י"א</u>
:בליל ראשון אומרים
.וּבְכֵן וַיְהִי בַּחֲצִי הַלַּיְלָה
.אָז רוֹב נִסִּים הִפְלֵאתָ בַּלַּיְלָה ,בְּראשׁ אַשְׁמוֹרֶת זֶה הַלַּיְלָה
.גֵּר צֶדֶק נִצַּחְתּוֹ כְּנֶחֱלַק לוֹ לַיְלָה ,וַיְהִי בַּחֲצִי הַלַּיְלָה
.דַּנְתָּ מֶלֶךְ גְּרָר בַּחֲלוֹם הַלַּיְלָה ,הִפְחַדְתָּ אֲרַמִּי בְּאֶמֶשׁ לַיְלָה
.וַיָּשַׂר יִשְׂרָאֵל לְמַלְאָךְ וַיּוּכַל לוֹ לַיְלָה ,וַיְהִי בַּחֲצִי הַלַּיְלָה
זֶרַע בְּכוֹרֵי פַתְרוֹס מָחַצְתָּ בַּחֲצִי הַלַּיְלָה ,חֵילָם לֹא מָצְאוּ בְּקוּמָם בַּלַּיְלָה ,טִיסַת נְגִיד חֲרֹשֶׁת סִלִּיתָ בְּכוֹכְבֵי
.לַיְלָה ,וַיְהִי בַּחֲצִי הַלַּיְלָה
יָעַץ מְחָרֵף לְנוֹפֵף אִוּוּי ,הוֹבַשְׁתָּ פְגָרָיו בַּלַּיְלָה ,כָּרַע בֵּל וּמַצָּבוֹ בְּאִישׁוֹן לַיְלָה ,לְאִישׁ חֲמוּדוֹת נִגְלָה רָז
.חֲזוֹת לַיְלָה ,וַיְהִי בַּחֲצִי הַלַּיְלָה

---

[42] http://worldatnature.com. Accessed 3/30/2022.

מִשְׂתַּכֵּר בִּכְלֵי קֹדֶשׁ נֶהֱרַג בּוֹ בַּלַּיְלָה ,נוֹשַׁע מִבּוֹר אֲרָיוֹת פּוֹתֵר בִּעֲתוּתֵי לַיְלָה ,שֹׂנְאָה נָטַר אֲגָגִי וְכָתַב סְפָרִים בַּלַּיְלָה ,וַיְהִי בַּחֲצִי הַלַּיְלָה.

עוֹרַרְתָּ נִצְחֲךָ עָלָיו בְּנֶדֶד שְׁנַת לַיְלָה .פּוּרָה תִדְרוֹךְ לְשׁוֹמֵר מַה מִלַּיְלָה ,צָרַח כַּשׁוֹמֵר וְשָׂח אָתָא בֹקֶר וְגַם לַיְלָה ,וַיְהִי בַּחֲצִי הַלַּיְלָה.

קָרֵב יוֹם אֲשֶׁר הוּא לֹא יוֹם וְלֹא לַיְלָה ,רָם הוֹדַע כִּי לְךָ הַיּוֹם אַף לְךָ הַלַּיְלָה ,שׁוֹמְרִים הַפְקֵד לְעִירְךָ כָּל הַיּוֹם וְכָל הַלַּיְלָה ,תָּאִיר כְּאוֹר יוֹם חֶשְׁכַּת לַיְלָה ,וַיְהִי בַּחֲצִי הַלַּיְלָה.

May the blessing of the LORD be upon you when you come together for your Seder. Celebrate the Passover remembering the salvation that the LORD granted to His people Israel. Amen.